# Revelation

## A Metaphysical Interpretation

## Rev. James R. D. Yeaw, D.Div., Editor

## Unity Spiritual Center

First Edition, 2017
Library of Congress Cataloging-in-Publication Data
Yeaw, James
Revelation: A Metaphysical Interpretation
 179 P. cm

Includes index

ISBN-13: 978-1542891189

ISBN-10: 1542891183

1.      New Testament 2.  Metaphysical Bible Interpretation

# Forward

A few years ago Ed Raybel developed a set of lessons for the ministerial education program of the Unity School of Christianity. These lessons were radically different than the usual story of doom and gloom based on the work of John Nelson Darby in the 19th century. Revelation was never meant to be a prophecy of the end of the world, but is, rather, an allegory of living the spiritual life, which all people in all times can benefit from.

According to this allegory, the return of Jesus and the raising of saints to meet him "in the air" in the "rapture," is the Christ becoming alive in those who have been "born again". This is the awareness of spirit, and the meeting of the Christ "in spirit."

The "tribulation" is spiritual awareness, in which God has only just "begun to reign," as we battle the "dragon" of bad habits, the "beast" of worldliness trying to tempt us back, and the "false prophet" of fear in our lives. When we have won the "battle" against these dark forces, then, in the language of revelation, their "Babylon" has fallen. Then there is great rejoicing in heaven, and we live in the "millennium," the "thousand" or perfect and holy years. It is the kingdom of heaven, when worldliness and temptation no longer assail us. We have reached the stage where, although we are still in the world, we are not of the world. "1000" does not mean the next number after 999, but according to the numerology of Revelation, it means "perfect and holy."

The lessons discuss these, and many other fascinating interpretations. It brings the Book of Revelation alive for you, for me, and for all humanity.

The original material has been reorganized with future discussion and explanation of the chakras, the energy centers that John called "churches." These materials have been refined for use in classes, such as those presented at Unity Spiritual Center.

Rev. James Yeaw, D.D., editor

# Contents

Forward ........................................................................................... iii

Chapter 1 - Background .................................................................. 1

Chapter 2 – Interpretation ............................................................. 7

Chapter 3 – Metaphysical Interpretation .................................. 23

Chapter 4 – The Chakras and Aura ............................................ 29

Chapter 5 – The Introduction to Revelation ............................ 37

Chapter 6 - The Message to Ephesus ....................................... 41

Chapter 7 - The Message to Smyrna ......................................... 47

Chapter 8 - The Message to Pergamum .................................... 55

Chapter 9 - The Message to Thyateira ...................................... 61

Chapter 10 – The Message to Sardis ......................................... 67

Chapter 11 – The Message to Philadelphia .............................. 73

Chapter 12 – The Message to Laodicea .................................... 81

Chapter 13 –A Scene in Heaven ................................................ 87

Chapter 14 – The Book with Seven Seals ................................. 91

Chapter 15 – The Angel and the Little Book ........................... 99

Chapter 16 – The Beast and the Bottomless Pit ..................... 103

Chapter 17 – The Downfall of Babylon .................................. 111

Appendix I – Symbolism ............................................................ 121

Index ............................................................................................ 127

# Chapter 1 - Background

Anyone who reads the book of Revelation for the first time and then asks seriously what it is all about will find the answer most elusive. Why is it even in the Bible? It almost was not selected as a book in the canon of the New Testament. Where are we supposed to get out of it? Why are there so many different explanations of it?

It is no secret that the Revelation of John has been a very controversial book. Not only does it elicit widely divergent interpretations.

The book of Revelation or The Apocalypse of John is the last canonical book of the New Testament in the Bible. It is the only biblical book that is wholly composed of apocalyptic literature. The book is frequently called "The book of Revelations" or simply "Revelations"; however, the title found on some of the earliest manuscripts is "The Apocalypse/Revelation of John", and the most common title found on later manuscripts is "The Apocalypse/ Revelation of the theologian"[1].

The first sentence of the book, *The Revelation of Jesus Christ ... unto his servant John*, is also sometimes used as a title." The Revelation of Jesus Christ, which God gave unto him, to shew unto his servants things which must shortly come to pass; and he sent and signified it by his angel unto his servant John..."[2]

After a short introduction,[3] it contains an account of the author, who identifies himself as John, and of two visions that he received on the isle of Patmos. The first vision,[4] related by "one like unto the Son of man, clothed with a garment down to the foot, and girt about the paps with a golden girdle", speaking with

---

[1] Nestle-Aland. *Novum Testamentum Graece*. 27th ed. Deutsche Bibelgesellschaft, Druck: 1996.
[2] King James Version
[3] 1:1-10
[4] 1:11-3:22

"a great voice, as of a trumpet", are statements addressed to the seven churches of Asia. The second vision comprising the rest of the book[5] begins with "a door opened in heaven" and describes the end of the world—involving the final rebellion by Satan at Armageddon, final defeat of Satan, and the restoration of peace to the world.

Revelation is considered one of the most controversial and most difficult books of the Bible, with many diverse interpretations of the meanings of the various names and events in the account. Protestant founder Martin Luther considered Revelation to be "neither apostolic nor prophetic" and stated that "Christ is neither taught nor known in it".

In the fourth century, St. John Chrysostom and other bishops argued against including this book in the New Testament canon, chiefly because of the difficulties of interpreting it and the danger for abuse. Christians in Syria also reject it because of the Montanists'[6] heavy reliance on it. In the 9th century, it was included with the *Apocalypse of Peter* among "disputed" books in the *Stichometry* of St. Nicephorus, Patriarch of Constantinople. In the end it was included in the accepted canon, although it remains the only book of the New Testament that is not read within the Divine Liturgy of the Eastern Orthodox Church.

## Authorship - discussed in the text

The author of Revelation identifies himself several times as "John".[7] The author also states that he was in exile on the island of Patmos when he received his first vision.[8] As a result the author of Revelation is referred to as John of Patmos. John explicitly

---

[5] Chapters 4-22

[6] **Montanism**, known by its adherents as the New Prophecy, was an early Christian movement of the late 2nd century, later referred to by the name of its founder, Montanus. Although it came to be labelled a heresy, the movement held similar views about the basic tenets of Christian doctrine to those of the wider Christian Church.

[7] 1:1, 4, 9; 22:8

[8] 1:9; 4:1-2

addresses Revelation to seven churches of Asia Minor: Ephesus, Smyrna, Pergamum, Thyatira, Sardis, Philadelphia, and Laodicea.[9] All of these sites are located in what is now Turkey.

Traditional views held that John the Apostle — considered to have written the Gospel and epistles by the same name — was exiled on Patmos in Aegean archipelago during the reign of Emperor Domitian, and that he wrote the Revelation there. Those in favor of a single common author point to similarities between the Gospel and Revelation. For example, both works are soteriological, referring to Jesus as a lamb, and possess a high Christology, referring to Jesus as "Lord of lords", and God's son. What is most telling, however, is that only in the Gospel of John and in Revelation is Jesus referred to as "the Word of God".

## Authorship - early views

A number of Church Fathers weighed in on the authorship of Revelation. Justin Martyr avows his belief in its apostolic origin. Irenaeus (178CE) assumes it as a conceded point. At the end of the 2nd century, we find it accepted at Antioch, by Theophilus, and in Africa by Tertullian. At the beginning of the third century, it is adopted by Clement of Alexandria and by Origen, later by Methodius, Cyprian, and Lactantius, Dionysius of Alexandria (247CE) rejected it, upon doctrinal rather than critical grounds. Eusebius (315CE) suspended his judgement, hesitating between the external and internal evidence. Some canons, especially in the Eastern Church, rejected the book, while most others included it.

## Authorship - modern views

Although the traditional view still has many adherents, many modern scholars believe that John the Apostle, John the Evangelist, and John of Patmos refer to three separate individuals. Certain lines of evidence suggest that John of Patmos wrote only

---

[9] 1:4, 11

Revelation, not the Gospel of John nor the Epistles of John. For one, the author of Revelation identifies himself as "John" several times, but the author of the Gospel of John never identifies himself directly. While both works liken Jesus to a lamb, they consistently use different words for lamb — the Gospel uses *amnos*, Revelation uses *arnion*. Lastly, the Gospel is written in nearly flawless Greek, but Revelation contains grammatical errors and stylistic abnormalities which indicate its author may not have been as familiar with the Greek language as the Gospel's author.

Dating

According to early tradition, the writing of this book took place near the very end of Domitian's reign, around 95 or 96CE. Others contend for an earlier date, 68 or 69, in the reign of Nero or shortly thereafter. Those who are in favor of the later date appeal to the external testimony of the Christian father Irenaeus (d. 185CE), who received information relative to this book from those who had seen John face to face. He says that the Apocalypse "was seen no very long time since, but almost in our day, towards the end of Domitian's reign", who according to Eusebius had started the persecution referred to in the book. However, some recent scholars dispute that the book is situated in a time of ongoing persecution and have also doubted the reality of a large-scale Domitian persecution. There is no reference to such a persecution before Eusebius.

**Chronology of Revelation**

Revelation is divided into seven cycles of events, with the number seven also appearing frequently as a symbol within the Book of Revelation. The chapters of Revelation present a series of events, full of imagery and metaphor, which detail the chronology of God's judgement on the world.

Exact interpretations of the Chronology of Revelation vary extensively. Literal biblical scholars often see the events portrayed as a "laundry list," to be checked off one by one as the time of Revelation grows near. Others feel that the many images in Revelation are figurative or perhaps even commentaries on the world during the time when Revelation was written.

# Chapter 2 – Interpretation

Revelation has a wide variety of interpretations, ranging from the message that we should have faith that God will prevail (*symbolic*), to complex end time scenarios (*futurist*),[10] [11] to the views of critics who deny any spiritual value to Revelation at all.[12] Some even suggest that its message is from a delusional mind.[13] Some of the various interpretations follow:

**Preterist View**

Preterism holds that the contents of Revelation constitute a prophecy of events that were fulfilled in the first century.[14] Preterist interpretations generally identify either Jerusalem or the Roman Empire as the persecutor of the Church and it is "Babylon," the "Mother of Harlots". They see Armageddon as God's judgment on the Jews, carried out by the Roman army, which is identified as "the beast". It sees Revelation being fulfilled in 70CE, thereby bringing the full presence of God to dwell with all humanity. Some preterists see the second half of Revelation as changing focus to Rome, its persecution of Christians, and the fall of the Roman Empire. It also holds that the Emperor Nero was possibly the number of the beast mentioned in the book as his

---

[10] Robert J. Karris (ed.) *The Collegeville Bible Commentary* Liturgical Press, 1992 p. 1296.
[11] Ken Bowers, *Hiding in Plain Sight*, Cedar Fort, 2000 p. 175.
[12] Carl Gustav Jung in *Memories Dream Reflections* said "I will not discuss the transparent prophecies of the Book of Revelation because no one believes in them and the whole subject is felt to be an embarrassing one."
[13] Rami Shapiro *Angelic Way* New York: BlueBridge (2009) p.133 asks, "What are we to make of the myth in Revelation? If Satan is the misdirected energy of the ego-centered mind, used not to transcend itself but to entrench itself all the more deeply in the dualistic 'I versus them' mind-set, then the book of Revelation is the classic mythic articulation of just how violent that mind-set and worldview can become."
[14] "The Whore of Babylon". Catholic Answers.
http://www.catholic.com/library/Whore_of_Babylon.asp. Retrieved 2007-05-11.

name equals 666 in Hebrew,[15] if using the Greek spelling of Nero's name (Neron Caesar), but using the Hebrew symbols with their assigned numeric values.[16]

**Futurist View**

The futurist view assigns all or most of the prophecy to the future, shortly before the second coming; especially when interpreted in conjunction with Daniel, Isaiah,[17] and Thessalonians.[18]

Futurist interpretations generally predict a resurrection of the dead and a rapture of the living, wherein all true Christians and those who have not reached an age of accountability are gathered to Jesus at the time God's kingdom comes on earth. They also believe a tribulation will occur - a seven year period of time when Christians will experience worldwide persecution and martyrdom, and be purified and strengthened by it. Futurists differ on when believers will be raptured. There are three primary views:

1. before the tribulation
2. near or at the midpoint of the tribulation.
3. at the end of the tribulation.

Pretribulationists believe that all Christians then alive will be taken up to meet Jesus before the Tribulation begins. In this manner, Christians are "kept" from the Tribulation, much as Noah was removed before God judged the antediluvian world.

Midtribulationists believe that the rapture of the faithful will occur approximately halfway through the Tribulation, after it begins but before the worst part of it occurs. Some midtribulationists, particularly those holding to a "pre-wrath

---

[15] "Apocalypse". Catholic Encyclopedia.
http://www.newadvent.org/cathen/01594b.htm. Retrieved 2007-05-11.
[16] An ancient method known as gematria
[17] 2:11-22
[18] 4:15-5:11

rapture" of the church, believe that God's wrath is poured out during a "Great Tribulation" that is limited to the last 3½ years of the Tribulation, after believers have been caught up to Christ.

Post-tribulationists believe that Christians will not be taken up into Heaven, but will be received into the Kingdom at the end of the Tribulation.

All three views hold that Christians will return with Jesus at the end of the Tribulation. Proponents of all three views also generally portray Israel as unwittingly signing a seven year peace treaty with the Antichrist, which initiates the seven year Tribulation. Many also tend to view the Antichrist as head of a revived Roman Empire, but the geographic location of this empire is unknown. Hal Lindsey suggests that this revived Roman Empire will be centered in Western Europe, with Rome as its capital. Tim LaHaye promotes the belief that Babylon will be the capital of a worldwide empire. Joel Richardson and Walid Shoebat have both recently written books proposing a revived eastern Roman Empire, which will fall with the boundaries of the Ottoman Empire.

The futurist view was first proposed by two Catholic writers, Manuel Lacunza and Ribera. Lacunza wrote under the pen name "Ben-Ezra", and his work was banned by the Catholic Church.

John Nelson Darby (1800-1882) was trained at Trinity College in Dublin, but became dissatisfied with institutional Christianity and its various denominations. At the age of 28 he started an association devoted to Christian evangelism. By 1930 the group was given the name "Plymouth Brethren."

Darby developed his seven-age dispensationalism. By 1835 he added "secret rapture," and gradually added dispensations up to 1838. A study of the Brethrens' proceedings reveals that their path was a rocky one, full of dissension and acrimony. Napoleon

Noel's *The History of the Brethren*[19] documents one of the most contentious histories imaginable for a Christian organization. Darby ran his organization with an iron hand, and was ruthless when someone contradicted him on a finer point of his doctrine.

The doctrine has grown in popularity in the 19th and 20th centuries through books about the "rapture" by authors like Hal Lindsey, and the more recent *Left Behind* novels by Jerry Jenkins and Tim LaHaye. There are also movies that have done much to popularize this school of thought. The *Scofield Reference Bible* also added to the popularity.[20]

The various views on tribulation are actually a subset of theological interpretations on the Millennium, mentioned in Revelation 20. There are three main interpretations:

1. Premillennialism
2. Amillennialism
3. Postmillennialism.

Premillennialism believes that Jesus will return to the earth, bind Satan, and reign for a literal thousand years on earth with Jerusalem as his capital. Thus Christ returns before the thousand years mentioned in chapter 20.

There are some that say that some form of premillennialism is thought to be the oldest millennial view in church history.[21] Actually there is evidence of the opposite. Louis Berkhof in *The History of Christian Doctrines*[22] states:

---

[19] Noel, Napoleon *The History of the Brethren* W. F. Knapp, 1935
[20] Seven age dispensationalism greatly appeals to the "Greek linear thinking" that characterizes the modern West, but has the outstanding weakness of connecting concretized aspects of Torah, prophets, epistles, gospels, and apocalyptic literature as if they were a single literary genre and without taking into account the cultural differences, let alone biblical contexts, in which each of these were set. The desire to have definite answers overcame all the rules of good biblical hermeneutics.
[21] Erickson, Millard J. (1982). *Contemporary Options in Eschatology*. Baker Book House. p. 94-95
[22] *Louis Berkhof, The History of Christian Doctrines, p. 262*

*"But it is not correct to say, as premillenarians do, that it was generally accepted in the first three centuries. The truth of the matter is that the adherents of this doctrine were a rather limited number. There is no trace of it in Clement of Rome, Ignatius, Polycarp, Tatian, Athenogoras, Theophilus, Clement of Alexandria, Origen, Dionysius, and other important church fathers."*

And Phillip Schaff in *History of the Christian Church*[23] states:

*"Among the Apostolic Fathers, Barnabas is the first and the only one who expressly teaches a pre-millennial reign of Christ on earth. He considers the Mosaic history of the creation a type of six ages of labor for the world, each lasting a thousand years, and of a millennium of rest; since with God "one day is as a thousand years." The millennial Sabbath on earth will be followed by an eighth and eternal day in a new world, of which the Lord's Day (called by Barnabas "the eighth day") is the type."*

So it is that in Amillennialism, the traditional view for Roman Catholicism, that the thousand years mentioned are not a literal thousand years, but is figurative for what is now the church age, usually, the time between Jesus' first ascension and second coming. This view is often associated with Augustine of Hippo. Amillennialists differ on the time frame of the millennium. Some say it started with Pentecost, others say it started with the fulfillment of Jesus' prophecy regarding the destruction of the temple in Jerusalem, and other starting points have also been proposed. Whether this eschatology is the result of caesaropapism, which may have also been the reason that premillennialism was condemned, is sharply disputed.

---

[23] *Phillip Schaff – History of the Christian Church Vol. II, p. 617*

Postmillennialism believes that Jesus will return after a literal/figurative thousand years, in which the world will have essentially become a Christendom. This view was held by Jonathan Edwards.

Robert Price refutes these millenialist and tribulationalist views in his book, *Apocalypse: How the Christian Church was Left Behind*.[24] Price explains how the various views of the Rapture, the Second Coming, the Antichrist, Messianic Prophecy, and most devastatingly, the fact the New Testament sets a first-century timeline for those early Christians that thought Jesus would return.

## Eastern Orthodox view

Eastern Orthodoxy treats the text as simultaneously describing contemporaneous events and as prophecy of events to come, for which the contemporaneous events were a form of foreshadow. It rejects attempts to determine, before the fact, if the events of Revelation are occurring by mapping them onto present-day events, taking to heart the Scriptural warning against those who proclaim "He is here!" prematurely. Instead, the book is seen as a warning to be spiritually and morally ready for the end times, whenever they may come "as a thief in the night", but they will come at the time of God's choosing, not something that can be precipitated nor trivially deduced by mortals.[25]

Book of Revelation is the only book of the New Testament that is not read during services by the Eastern Orthodox Church. In the Coptic Orthodox Church, the whole Book of Revelation is read during Apocalypse Night or Bright Saturday (the eve of the Resurrection).

---

[24] Price, Robert *Apocalypse: How the Christian Church was Left Behind*. Prothotheus Books, 2007

[25] Averky (Taushev), Archbishop (1996-Eng. tr. Fr. Seraphim Rose), *The Apocalypse: In the Teachings of Ancient Christianity*, Platina CA: St. Herman of Alaska Brotherhood.

## Paschal Liturgical View

This view, which has found expression among both Catholic and Protestant theologians, considers the liturgical worship, particularly the Easter rites, of early Christianity as background and context for understanding the Book of Revelation's structure and significance. This perspective is explained in *The Paschal Liturgy and the Apocalypse*[26] by an Episcopal scholar, and in *The Lamb's Supper: The Mass as Heaven on Earth*,[27] in which he states that Revelation in form is structured after creation, fall, judgment and redemption. Those who hold this view say that the Temple's destruction (70CE) had a profound effect on the Jewish people, not only in Jerusalem but among the Greek-speaking Jews of the Mediterranean.[28] They believe The Book of Revelation provides insight into the early Eucharist, saying that it is the new Temple worship in the New Heaven and Earth. The idea of the Eucharist as a foretaste of the heavenly banquet is also explored by British Methodist Geoffrey Wainwright in his book *Eucharist and Eschatology*.[29]

## Radical Discipleship View

The radical discipleship view asserts that the Book of Revelation is best understood as a handbook for radical discipleship; i.e. how to remain faithful to the spirit and teachings of Jesus and avoid simply assimilating to surrounding society. In this view, the primary agenda of the book is to expose the worldly powers as impostors which seek to oppose the ways of God. The chief temptation for Christians in the first century, and today, is to fail to hold fast to the non-violent teachings and example of Jesus

---

[26] Shepherd, Massey H. *The Paschal Liturgy and the Apocalypse, 2004*
[27] Hahn, Scott *The Lamb's Supper: The Mass as Heaven on Earth, 1999*
[28] Scott Hahn, *The Lamb's Supper: The Mass as Heaven on Earth*,. New York, NY: Doubleday, 1999.
[29] Wainwright, Geoffrey *Eucharist and Eschatology*(Oxford University Press, 1980).[29]

and instead be lured into unquestioning adoption of worldly, national or cultural values, imperialism being the most dangerous and insidious. This perspective, closely related to liberation theology, draws on the approach of Bible scholars such as Ched Myers, William Stringfellow, Richard Horsley, Daniel Berrigan, Wes Howard-Brook,[30] and Joerg Reiger.

### Aesthetic and Literary View

Many literary writers and theorists have contributed to a wide range of views about the origins and purpose of the Book of Revelation. Some of these writers have no connection with established Christian faiths but, nevertheless, found in Revelation a source of inspiration. Revelation has been approached from Hindu philosophy and Jewish Midrash. Others have pointed to aspects of composition which have been ignored such as the similarities of prophetic inspiration to modern poetic inspiration, or the parallels with Greek drama. In recent years theories have arisen which concentrate upon how readers and texts interact to create meaning and are less interested in what the original author intended.

Charles Cutler Torrey taught Semitic languages at Yale. His lasting contribution has been to show how much more meaningful prophets, such as the scribe of Revelation, are when treated as poets first and foremost. He felt this was a point often lost sight of because most English bibles render everything in prose.[31] Poetry was also the reason John never directly quoted the older prophets. Had he done so, he would have had to use

---

[30] Howard-Brook, Wes; Gwyther, Anthony (1999). *Unveiling Empire: Reading Revelation Then and Now*. Orbis Books

[31] Charles C. Torrey *The Apocalypse of John* New Haven: Yale University Press (1958). Christopher R. North in his *The Second Isaiah* London: OUP (1964) p. 23 says of Torrey's earlier Isaiah theory, "Few scholars of any standing have accepted his theory." This is the general view of Torrey's theories. However, Christopher North goes on to cite Torrey on 20 major occasions and many more minor ones in the course of his book. So, Torrey must have had some influence and poetry is the key.

their Hebrew poetry whereas he wanted to write his own. Torrey insisted Revelation had originally been written in Aramaic.[32] This was why the surviving Greek translation was written in such a strange idiom. It was a literal translation that had to comply with the warning in Revelation 22[33] that the text must not be corrupted in any way. According to Torrey, the story is that "The Fourth Gospel was brought to Ephesus by a Christian fugitive from Palestine soon after the middle of the first century. It was written in Aramaic." Later, the Ephesians claimed this fugitive had actually been the beloved disciple himself. Subsequently, this John was banished by Nero and died on Patmos after writing Revelation. Torrey argued that until 80CE, when Christians were expelled from the synagogues,[34] the Christian message was always first heard in the synagogue and, for cultural reasons, the evangelist would have spoken in Aramaic, else "he would have had no hearing."[35] Torrey showed how the three major songs in Revelation[36] each fall naturally into four regular metrical lines plus a coda.[37] Other dramatic moments in Revelation[38], where the terrified people cry out to be hidden, behave in a similar way.[39]

Christina Rossetti was a Victorian poet who believed the sensual excitement of the natural world found its meaningful purpose in death and in God.[40] Her *The Face of the Deep* is a meditation upon the Apocalypse. In her view, what Revelation has

---

[32] *Apocalypse of John* p. 7
[33] Revelation 22:8
[34] *Apocalypse of John* p. 37
[35] *Apocalypse of John* p. 8
[36] the new song, the song of Moses and the Lamb and the chorus at 19: 6-8
[37] *Apocalypse of John* p. 137
[38] 6:16
[39] *Apocalypse of John* p. 140
[40] "Flowers preach to us if we will hear," begins her poem 'Consider the lilies of the field' *Goblin Market* London: Oxford University Press (1913) p. 87

to teach is patience.[41] Patience is the closest to perfection the human condition allows.[55] Her book, which is largely written in prose, frequently breaks into poetry or jubilation, much like Revelation itself. The relevance of John's visions[42] belongs to Christians of all times as a continuous present meditation. Such matters are eternal and outside of normal human reckoning. "That winter which will be the death of Time has no promise of termination. Winter that returns not to spring ... - who can bear it?"[57] She dealt deftly with the vengeful aspects of John's message. "A few are charged to do judgment; everyone without exception is charged to show mercy."[43] Her conclusion is that Christians should see John as "representative of all his brethren" so they should "hope as he hoped, love as he loved."[44]

Recently, aesthetic and literary modes of interpretation have developed, which focus on Revelation as a work of art and imagination, viewing the imagery as symbolic depictions of timeless truths and the victory of good over evil. Elisabeth Schuessler Fiorenza wrote *Revelation: Vision of a just world* from the viewpoint of rhetoric.[45] Accordingly, Revelation's meaning is partially determined by the way John goes about saying things, partially by the context in which readers receive the message and partially by its appeal to something beyond logic. It is Professor Schuessler Fiorenza's view that Revelation has particular relevance today as a liberating message to disadvantaged groups.

---

[41] Ms Rossetti remarks that patience is a word which does not occur in the Bible until the New Testament, as if the usage first came from Christ's own lips. Christina Rossetti *The Face of the Deep* London: SPCK (1892) p. 115

[42] 'vision' lends the wrong emphasis as Ms Rossetti sought to minimize the distinction between John's experience and that of others. She quoted 1 John 3:24 "He abideth in us, by the Spirit which he hath given us" to show that when John says, "I was in the Spirit" it is not exceptional.

[43] *The Face of the Deep* p. 292

[44] *The Face of the Deep* p. 495

[45] Elisabeth Schuessler Fiorenza *Revelation: Vision of a just world* Edinburgh: T&T Clark (1993). The book seems to have started life as *Invitation to the Book of Revelation* Garden City: Doubleday (1981)

John's book is a vision of a just world, not a vengeful threat of world-destruction. Her view that Revelation's message is not gender-based has caused dissent. She says we are to look behind the symbols rather than make a fetish out of them. Tina Pippin puts an opposing view[46] that John writes "horror literature" and "the misogyny which underlies the narrative is extreme". Professor Schuessler Fiorenza would seem to be saying John's book is more like science fiction; it does not foretell the future but uses present-day concepts to show how contemporary reality could be very different.

D. H. Lawrence took an opposing, pessimistic view of Revelation in the final book he wrote, *Apocalypse*.[47] He saw the language which Revelation used as being bleak and destructive; a 'death-product'. Instead, he wanted to champion a public-spirited individualism (which he identified with the historical Jesus supplemented by an ill-defined cosmic consciousness) against its two natural enemies. One of these he called "the sovereignty of the intellect"[48] which he saw in a technology-based totalitarian society. The other enemy he styled "vulgarity"[49] and that was what he found in Revelation. "It is very nice if you are poor and not humble ... to bring your enemies down to utter destruction, while you yourself rise up to grandeur. And nowhere does this happen so splendiferously than in Revelation."[50] His specific aesthetic objections to Revelation were that its imagery was unnatural and that phrases like "the wrath of the Lamb" were

---

[46] Tina Pippin *Death & Desire: The rhetoric of gender in the Apocalypse of John* Louisville: Westminster-John Knox (1993) p. 105
[47] D. H. Lawrence *Apocalypse* London: Martin Secker (1932) published posthumously with an introduction (p. v - xli) by Richard Aldington which is an integral part of the text.
[48] *Apocalypse* p. xxiii
[49] *Apocalypse* p. 6
[50] Apocalypse p. 11 Lawrence did not consider how these two types of Christianity (good and bad in his view) might be related other than as opposites. He noted the difference meant that the John who wrote a gospel could not be the same John that wrote Revelation.

"ridiculous". He saw Revelation as comprising two discordant halves. In the first, there was a scheme of cosmic renewal "great Chaldean sky-spaces" which he quite liked. Then the book hinged around the birth of the baby messiah. After that, "flamboyant hate and simple lust ... for the end of the world." Lawrence coined the term "Patmossers" to describe those Christians who could only be happy in paradise if they knew their enemies were suffering hell.

James Morgan Pryse was an esoteric gnostic who saw Revelation as a western version of the Hindu theory of the Chakra. He began his work, "The purpose of this book is to show that the Apocalypse is a manual of spiritual development and not, as conventionally interpreted, a cryptic history or prophecy". On this theory, Revelation is a 'pilgrim's progress' of individual spiritual development. That individual, starting out as "I, John", goes through the difficult stages of development as "the sacrificed Lamb", and reaches his goal as "Iesous the Christos". It assumes the impulse to begin such a journey comes from a spark inside the individual, not from any book. James Pryse does not merely attempt to explain what John's language is about but seeks to show that such a message could only be conveyed in the language the book used. Paradoxically, on this view, Revelation was written to conceal; making the heart of the people fat. Such a path of spiritual development is difficult, hence the wealth of negative and destructive imagery employed and the appeal to Jesus to "come quickly" so that a process which would otherwise take many lifetimes can be completed using intuition and enlightenment. Those who 'die the death' are simply being put back into the pool of life to try again.

Whilst such diverse theories have not yet commanded widespread acceptance, they may throw light upon passages of Revelation which present difficulties. For example, the imagery surrounding the woman clothed with the sun[51] (Rev 12:1) may be easier to understand if one looks a little outside of Christian theology. As Christopher Rowland has said, "there are always going to be loose threads which refuse to be woven into the fabric as a whole. The presence of the threads which stubbornly refuse to be incorporated into the neat tapestry of our world-view does not usually totally undermine that view."[52]

**The Historical-Critical view**

The historical-critical method treats Revelation as a text and attempts to understand Revelation in its first century historical context within the genre of Jewish and Christian apocalyptic literature.

This approach considers the text as an address to seven historical communities in Asia Minor. Under this view, assertions that "the time is near" are to be taken literally by those communities. Consequently the work is viewed as a warning not to conform to contemporary Greco-Roman society which John "unveils" as beastly, demonic and subject to divine judgment. There is further information on these topics in the entries on higher criticism and apocalyptic literature.

The acceptance of Revelation into the canon is itself the result of a historical process, essentially no different from the career of other texts. The eventual exclusion of other contemporary apocalyptic literature from the canon may throw light on the unfolding historical processes of what was officially considered orthodox, what was heterodox, what was even heretical. Interpretation of meanings and imagery are anchored in what the historical author intended and what his contemporary audience inferred; a message to Christians not to assimilate into the Roman imperial culture was John's central message. Thus, his

---

[51] 12:1
[52] Christopher Rowland *Revelation* London:Epworth (1993) p.5

letter (written in the apocalyptic genre) is pastoral in nature, and the symbolism of Revelation is to be understood entirely within its historical, literary and social context. Critics study the conventions of apocalyptic literature and events of the first century to make sense of what the author may have intended.

During a discussion about Revelation on 23 August 2006, Pope Benedict XVI remarked: "The seer of Patmos, identified with the apostle, is granted a series of visions meant to reassure the Christians of Asia amid the persecutions and trials of the end of the first century."[53]

## Esoteric View

The esoterist views Revelation as bearing multiple levels of meaning, the lowest being the literal. They see the book as delivering both a series of warnings for humanity and a detailed account of internal, spiritual processes of the individual soul.

The Gnostic Kabbalist believes that Revelation, like Genesis, is a very profound book of Kabbalistic symbolism. This view is held by teachers such as H.P. Blavatsky, Eliphas Levi, and Rudolf Steiner.

A zodiacal interpretation of Genesis and Revelation as alpha and omega is given in Anna P. Johnson *Tau: The key of heaven*[54] in which it is claimed the astrology practiced in Eden is the missing wisdom that would make prophecy and modern science completely compatible. Anna Johnson claimed that the two witnesses of Revelation are the male and female principles, that the norms of western society are wholly perverse, and that death could be overcome if the vagina was no longer 'prostituted' to sexual lust. In her theory, the human aging process and biblical animal sacrifice have both been needless human cringing before a fire-god demiurge. Creation and evolution can coexist because

---

[53] Pope Benedict: Read Book of Revelation as Christ's victory over evil - Catholic Online
[54] Anna P. Johnson Tau: *The key of Heaven* New York: Asa K Butts (1881)

evolution needs much shorter time periods if punctuated by periodic calamities brought about by the change of aeon which cause huge jumps in world development. It is one of these huge jumps which will make it possible for the elect to survive the passing away of the old earth.[55]

## Mystical and Metaphysical Views

Like the esoterist, the metaphysician view Revelation as bearing multiple levels of meaning, the lowest being literal. They see the book as a detailed account of internal, spiritual processes of the individual soul. We will explore Revelation from these viewpoints in the next chapter.

Before we go on, we make one more note about Revelation as apocalyptic literature.

The Revelation of St. John, along with Daniel in the Hebrew Scriptures, are apocalyptic. Apocalyptic literature is a genre of prophetical writing that developed in post-Exhilic Jewish culture popular among millennialist early Christians.

Apocalypse is a Greek word meaning "revelation", an unveiling or unfolding of things not previously known and which cannot be known apart from unveiling.[56] The apocalyptic literature of Judaism and Christianity embraces a considerable time period, from the centuries following the exile to Babylon down to the close of the middle ages.

## Edgar Cayce

An example of metaphysical interpretation is found in the writings of Edgar Cayce. He believed that the Bible is the symbolic account of the fall of the human soul from its divine origins and restoration of the human soul to heaven (as symbolically

---

[55] Unlike most modern versions of this theory (for example Gordon Strachan *The Bible's Hidden Cosmology* Edinburgh: Floris 2005) Anna P. Johnson sees Revelation as the end of the known world, not merely a change of aeon.
[56] Gosweiler, Richard *Revelation, Pacific Study Series*, Melbourne, 1987, page 3

described in the Book of Revelation). In other words, Genesis is the symbolic testimony of humanity's fall from heavenly potential or paradise lost. Revelation is the symbolic testimony of humanity's restoration to heaven and paradise regained.

In the Book of Revelation, John records a vision he experiences, while dreaming or meditating. This vision contains symbolism; the same kind of symbolism one would see in a dream, a vision of the spirit world. In fact, the Book of Revelation contains the same symbolism found in the symbols in the Prophet Daniel's dream. All Biblical dreams, such as those of Joseph, Gideon, Daniel, Paul, and Peter, are very symbolic and therefore had a hidden spiritual meaning rather than a literal interpretation of the symbols.

During several of Cayce's journeys into the spirit realms, it is said that he was able to unlock the secrets to the symbolism in the Book of Revelation. He gave a large amount of information specifically for the purpose of discovering the book's hidden meaning.

Cayce described the true nature between humanity and God. Cayce revealed that humans have three different dimensions of awareness: the conscious mind, the subconscious mind and the superconscious mind. An important goal in everyone's life is to awaken our superconscious mind to attain what Cayce called at-one-ment with God.

The superconscious mind is called by many names by many religions in many different cultures. Some of these names are: Buddha consciousness, Christ consciousness, the Collective Mind, the Universal Mind, the Collective Unconsciousness, the Holy Spirit, Brahman, God, the Clear White Light, Allah, Higher Self, or the Mind of Christ.[57]

---

[57] Van Auken, John Edgar Cayce on the Revelation: A Study Guide for Spiritualizing Body and Mind ARE Press, 2000

# Chapter 3 – Metaphysical Interpretation

Although, as you have seen, there are other interpretations, there is much to learn about self and soul growth as we look at Revelation through the metaphysical or mystical lens.

## A Metaphysical Approach to the Bible

Most of us are affected or conditioned by the Bible. Whether we accept all or part of it as "gospel", we are surrounded by a culture that is filled with references to legal and ethical concepts from the Bible. To really understand our culture, we need to understand something about the Bible.

Many spiritually minded people have given up reading the Bible because they find it difficult to Understand and accept. But, there are approaches to the interpretation of the Bible that may help us to understand the hidden mystical tradition deep within it.

The Bible is an esoteric book, meaning that it contains hidden information in addition to the obvious, literal interpretation. In ancient times, only those in an inner circle were allowed to know the inner teachings.

There are several ways to begin to unlock the secrets hidden within the Bible. One of the most powerful ways is to translate the names of people and places from the original Hebrew, Greek, and Aramaic to English. This has been done for you in the *Metaphysical Bible Dictionary*.[58] Numbers and key words are also helpful.

The most important insight, however, is that the stories reflect inner experiences. The narratives appear to be historical events, but they are descriptive experiences of individuals, including ourselves. An example of this is Jesus' story of the Good Samaritan. The story is about us, lying at the side of the road,

---

[58] ---, *Metaphysical Bible Dictionary*, Unity Books, 2007

where life experiences seem to dump us. The priest representing religion, does help us. Neither does the Levite, representing legalism, mind-centered experiences. But, the one whom we rejected, the Samaritan, comes along, binds up our wounds and gives us shelter and healing.

As we have shown, the elements of the story represent our life and our experiences. Personalities represent conditions of consciousness and qualities of character. Often the names are changed, such as Abram to Abraham, representing new levels of consciousness.

There are many interpretations of the Bible and they are all valuable as they represent our individual life experiences. With an understanding of the meaning of numbers, allegory, symbolism, and names, coupled with the cultural and historic background of the writings, we can come to a deeper understanding of the text.

There are at least three levels of meaning in the Bible. The most obvious is the historical level. Secondly, there is the level of thought, or psychology, dealing with ethics or morals. The third level is spiritual, dealing with the development of or informing the soul.

The soul, according to Charles Fillmore, the founder of Unity, includes the conscious and subconscious minds. Soul makes the body, the body is the outer expression of the soul, and bodily health is in exact correspondence to the health of the soul. That phase of the soul named sub-consciousness, draws its life from both the earthly side of existence and the spiritual; it answers to both good and evil, light and darkness. It is this drawing of spiritual insight that is accomplished through meditation on sacred writings.

You may question why the Bible, and other sacred writings, were composed in this fashion. The interpretation is also always changing. Our individual spiritual journey is in sacred literature. We are the leading characters, the protagonist of the Bible.

We are not suggesting that there is not an historical significance to the Biblical stories. Many make more sense allegorically than literally, and we believe that history told as a story imparts a deeper message.

This way of interpretation, as well as our own cultural mythology makes the story accessible to all. No longer are the stories of the Hebrew Scriptures a story for the Hebrew people, they are stories with meaning for all people. It is not a national epic authored by many and compiled by the Jews in exile, it is the epic story of all humankind. It describes our journey to find salvation, the Holy Grail or illumination, whatever we seek. It is about finding the path, the decision to take it, the pitfalls along the way and the joys of accomplishment.

There are many books available to help us become familiar with metaphysical interpretation. Some of these books are:

- *Your Hope of Glory* by Elizabeth Sand Turner
- *Be Ye Transformed* by Elizabeth Sand Turner
- *Bible Mystery and Bible Meaning* by Thomas Troward
- *The Hidden Bible* by John P. Scott
- *The Hidden Mystery of the Bible* by Jack Ensign Addington
- *The Hidden Wisdom of the Bible* by Geoffrey Hodson
- *Idioms of the Bible Explained* by George M. Lamsa
- *The Metaphysical Bible Dictionary* by Unity'
- *The Revealing Word* by Charles Fillmore
- *New Age Bible Interpretation* by Corine Heline
- *Old Testament Light* by George M. Lamsa
- *Understanding the Kabbalah* by Edward Albertson
- *What the Bible Really Says* by Manfred Barthell
- *The Greatest Stories ever Told* by Neil Mence

In reading the Bible metaphysically, it is also important to understand the purpose of each of the 66 books. The following table provides you with a purpose statement. Not all of the books included in the Hebrew and Christian scriptures are to be interpreted metaphysically.

| Foundational Stories | Symbolic stories about the origins of the world, the first generations of humans, and the early years of the Hebrew people. (Genesis, parts of Exodus, Numbers and Deuteronomy). This material cannot be verified historically and must be looked at metaphysically. |
|---|---|

| Legal Codes | Collections of laws and instructions by which individuals are to live (Leviticus, parts of Exodus, Numbers and Deuteronomy). Not subject to metaphysical interpretation and apply to the culture of the Hebrew people prior to the time of Jesus. |
|---|---|
| Genealogies | Lists of relationships between people, either of successive generations or of different nations. (parts of Genesis, much of Numbers). |
| Annals | Semi-historical narratives of events. Focus is on political and military exploits and written as a national epic. Some portions are historical; others are stories to be interpreted metaphysically. (Joshua, Judges, I & II Samuel, I & II Kings) |
| Prophecy | Collections of words spoken to the people through prophets. (Isaiah, Jeremiah, Ezekiel...) |
| Psalms, Songs | Poetic lyrics of songs/hymns intended for communal worship or lament (Psalms, Lamentations) |
| Proverbs | Generalized sayings and aphorisms containing advice on how to live. (Proverbs) |
| Wisdom Literature | Inspirational stories (Job, Ruth...) |
| Apocalyptic | Symbolic narratives that interpret crisis to provide hope. (Daniel) This is subject to metaphysical interpretation. |

Christian scriptures also include various genres of literature:

| | |
|---|---|
| Gospels | Biographies of Jesus. Stories and events are highly symbolic and are subject to metaphysical interpretation (Matthew, Mark, Luke, and, especially, John. |
| Acts | A narrative about the beginnings and growth of early Christian communities. (Acts) |
| Letters | Letters addressing issues and situations arising in the early Jewish-Christian communities. Seven are known to be written by Paul. |
| Church Orders | Collections of instructions for governance of communities (I Timothy, Titus) |
| Testament | A document that gives a person's last wishes and instructions for successors (II Timothy, II Peter) |
| Homily, Sermon | A sermon that interprets other texts in reference to the Christ (Hebrews) |
| Wisdom | A collection of instructions on the Christian life (James). |
| Epistles | Letters intended as instructions (I & II Peter). |
| Apocalyptic | Symbolic visions and prophecies. It describes the unfoldment of the soul after an individual remembers the presence of the Christ (Revelation). |

# Chapter 4 – The Chakras and Aura

Before discussing revelation, there is another important subject to consider in that the book of Revelation is about energy centers.

Our physical body which is made up of matter or energy, in a solidified state. It is intertwined with our soul. The soul is also composed of energy, but not in a solidified state. The soul draws its energy from both the earthly side of existence and the spiritual. It is the amalgamation of various energies that makes up our soul, also called our subtle energy body.[59] This energy field which will be released upon death when this energy barrier weakens and ceases to exist. Energy is never still, it is constantly moving and flowing like water. It can never be destroyed as it can only be transformed. When the various energy paths crisscrosses one another it creates an energy vortex or an energy center, called a Chakra.

---

[59] According to *Bhagavad Gita*, one of the most sacred texts of Hinduism, the subtle body is composed of mind, intelligence and ego, which controls the physical body. It is also known in other different spiritual traditions: "the most sacred body" (*wujud al-aqdas*) and "true and genuine body" (*jism asli haqiqi*) in Sufism, "the diamond body" in Taoism and Vajrayana, "the light body" or "rainbow body" in Tibetan Buddhism, "the body of bliss" in Kriya Yoga, and "the immortal body" (*soma athanaton*) in Hermeticism.

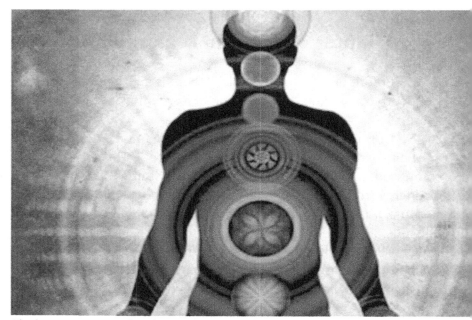

Chakra means a wheel or a disc, which is the eastern terminology for the energy vortices spinning in the body. These chakras or energy centers are formed by energy pathways crisscrossing each other and it is this energy that forms our subtle energy body. There are over 2000 chakras in the human body which are comprised of major and minor chakras. There are only seven major chakra points.

Around each physical body there is also an energy field known as the aura. It extends out from the physical body in seven layers. Some people can see the aura with all its colors, others can see a faint light, while some cannot see anything at all. The colors in our aura change depending on our state of health or our mood. The color and energy of the aura is produced by the chakras. They are wheels of bright color which spin totally in balance when we are healthy and happy. When we are in bad health or feeling distressed, the chakras spin out of balance and the colors dim.

Failure to deal with spiritual issues, which are also mental and emotional issues is likely to result in the manifestation of illness or dis-ease in the body. There is a link between how we live our lives, what we think, and our health.

Many spiritual groups and individual teachers have used their experience to help categorize the relationship between metaphysical issues and how they may manifest in the body. The seminal work in this area is the book *Heal Your Body*[60] by Louise Hay which lists common illnesses and diseases and suggests the possible metaphysical causes.

Our soul and our body is linked at the chakras. This link is already supported by the empirical and anecdotal evidence like "Science of Mind" and by teachers like Louise Hay; but also the scientific fact and the evidence continues to grow. This link between the soul and the energy centers has a far greater influence on our bodily health than previously believed by science.

## The Base or Root Chakra

The Base or Root Chakra is associated with the color red. This chakra is the grounding force that allows us to connect to the earth energies and empower ourselves. The physical Location is at the base of the spine and the purposes are kinesthetic feelings, and movement. The spiritual Lesson is about material world lessons. Physical dysfunctions associated with the

---

[60] Hay, Louise *Heal Your Body* Hay House, 2010

base chakra - lower back pain, sciatica, varicose veins, rectal tumors, depression, and immune related disorders.

Mental/Emotional Issues are survival, self-esteem, social order, security, family. The information stored in the base chakra include familial beliefs, superstitions, loyalty, instincts, physical pleasure or pain, touch and the area of Body Governed include the  spinal column, kidneys, legs, feet, rectum, and immune system.

## The Sacral Chakra

The Sacral Chakra is associated with the color orange. This chakra often offers us the opportunity to lessen our "control issues" and find a balance in our lives, teaching us to recognize that acceptance and rejection are not the only options in our relationships. The process of making changes in our life stream through our personal choices is a product of second chakra energy. A well-functioning sacral chakra helps one to maintain a healthy balanced existence. The physical location is the lower abdomen to the navel and the purpose is emotional connection. The spiritual lesson is creativity, manifestation, honoring relationships, and learning to "let go". Physical dysfunctions associated with sacral chakra - low back pain, sciatica, ob/gyn problems, pelvic pain, libido, and urinary problems. Mental/Emotional Issues are blame, guilt, money, sex, power, control, creativity, and morality. Information stored in sacral chakra include duality, magnetism, controlling patterns, and the emotional feelings of joy, anger, and fear. The area of body governed are the sexual organs, stomach, upper intestines, liver, gallbladder, kidney, pancreas, adrenal glands, spleen, and middle spine.

## The Solar Plexus Chakra

The Solar Plexus Chakra is associated with the color yellow. This is the area which defines our "self-esteem". The personality that develops during puberty is housed in this chakra...otherwise known as the "ego". Anyone experiencing dysfunction of the third chakra is having difficulty obtaining or maintaining "personal power". This intuitive chakra is where we get our "gut instincts" that signal us to do or not to do something. Strong self-esteem is a required for developing intuitive skills. The physical location is the solar plexus and the purpose is mental understanding of emotional life. The spiritual lesson is acceptance of your place in the life stream or self-love. Physical dysfunctions associated with solar plexus chakra include stomach ulcers, intestinal tumors, diabetes, pancreatitis, indigestion, anorexia, bulimia, hepatitis, cirrhosis, adrenal imbalances, arthritis, and colon diseases. Mental or emotional Issues are self-esteem, fear of rejection, oversensitivity to criticism, self-image fears, fears of our secrets being found out, and indecisiveness. Information stored in solar plexus chakra include personal power, personality, consciousness of self within the universe or our sense of belonging and knowing. The area of body governed is the upper abdomen, umbilicus to rib cage, liver, gallbladder, middle spine, spleen, kidney, adrenals, small intestines, and the stomach.

**The Heart Chakra**

The Heart Chakra is associated with the color green or pink. This love center of our human energy system is often the focus in bringing about a healing. Thus, the words "love heals all" have great truth. Hurtful situations that can affect our emotional being are divorce or separation, grief through death, emotional abuse, abandonment, and adultery. All of these are wounding to the heart chakra. Physical illnesses brought about by heartbreak require that an emotional healing occur along with the physical healing. Learning to love yourself is a powerful first step in securing a healthy fourth chakra. The "wounded child" resides in the heart chakra. The physical Location is the center of the chest and the purposes is emotional empowerment. The spiritual Lessons are forgiveness, unconditional love, letting go, trust, and compassion. Physical dysfunctions associated with the heart chakra include heart conditions, asthma, lung and breast cancers, thoracic spine, pneumonia, upper back, and shoulder problems. The mental/emotional Issues are love, compassion, confidence, inspiration, hope, despair, hate, envy, fear, jealousy, anger, and generosity. Information stored in heart chakra are connections or "heart strings" to those whom we love. The area of the body governed by the heart chakra are the  heart, circulatory system, blood, lungs, rib cage, diaphragm, thymus, breasts, esophagus, , shoulders, arms, and hands.

### The Throat Chakra

 The Throat Chakra is associated with the color sky blue. This chakra is our will center. The healthfulness of the fifth chakra is in relation to how honestly one expresses himself/herself. Lying violates the body and soul. We speak our choices with our voices or throats. All choices we make in our lives have consequences on an energetic level. Even choosing not to make a choice such as in repressing our anger (not speaking out) may manifest into laryngitis. We have all experienced that "lump in our throats" when we are at a crossroad of not knowing how to speak the right words in any given situation, perhaps even stuffing our own emotions. A challenge of the throat chakra is to express ourselves in the most truthful manner. Also to receive and assimilate information and seek only the truth. The physical Location is in the throat or neck region. Purposes include learning to take responsibility for one's own needs.

The spiritual Lesson is confession, surrender personal will to divine will, faith, and truthfulness over deceit. The physical dysfunctions associated with throat chakra are a sore throat, mouth ulcers, scoliosis, swollen glands, thyroid dysfunctions, laryngitis, voice problems, as well as gum or tooth problems. The mental/emotional Issues are personal expression, creativity, addiction, criticism, faith, choices in decision making, will, and lack of authority. The information stored in the throat chakra includes self-knowledge, truth, attitudes, hearing, taste, and smell. The area of the body governed is the throat, thyroid, trachea, neck vertebrae, mouth, teeth, gums, esophagus, parathyroid, and hyperchalemus.

## The Third Eye or Brow Chakra

 The Third Eye Chakra is associated with the color indigo. It is also often referred to as the "third eye" or the "mind center". It is our avenue to wisdom - learning from our experiences and putting them in perspective. Our ability to separate reality from fantasy or delusions is in connection with the healthfulness of this chakra. Achieving the art of detachment beyond "small mindedness" is accomplished through developing impersonal intuitive reasoning. It is through an open brow chakra that visual images are received. The physical location is in the center of the forehead and the purposes include action of ideas, insight, and mind development. The spiritual Lesson are understanding, reality check point, detachment, and an open mind. The physical dysfunctions associated with brow chakra are brain tumors, strokes, blindness, deafness, seizures, learning disabilities, spinal dysfunctions, panic, and depression. Mental/emotional Issues are fear of truth, discipline, judgement, evaluation, emotional intelligence, concept of reality, and confusion. The information stored in brow chakra - seeing a clear picture, symbolic or literal, wisdom, intuition, mental facilities, and intellect. The area of Body governed is the brain, neurological system, eyes, ears, nose, pituitary, and pineal glands.

## The Crown Chakra

 The Crown Chakra is associated with the color indigo or white. We use the seventh chakra as a tool to communicate with our spiritual nature. It is through this vortex that the life force is dispersed from the universe into the other six chakras. It has been referred to as our "God source". This terminology might be confusing to anyone who equates God with religious dogma. If so, we may choose to call it a spiritual connection or communicator. This chakra is often pictured as a lotus flower opening to allow spiritual awakening in an individual. The crown chakra could also be considered the well intuitive knowing is drawn from. The physical Location is the top of head and the purpose is intuitive knowing, connection to one's spirituality, and integration of the whole. The spiritual lessons are spirituality, and living in the present moment. The physical dysfunctions associated with crown chakra include mystical depression, diseases of the muscular system, skeletal system and the skin, chronic exhaustion not associated with physical ailments, as well as sensitivity to light, sound, or the environment. The mental/ emotional Issues are discovery of the divine, lack of purpose, loss of meaning or identity, trust, selflessness, humanitarianism, ability to see the bigger picture in the life stream, devotion, inspiration, values, and ethics. The information stored in crown chakra is a concept of the whole and the area of body governed is the top center of the head from the midline above the ears.

# Chapter 5 – The Introduction to Revelation

I.      Major Points
   - a. Metaphysical significance of God designated as One.
   - b. Metaphysical meaning of the twenty-four elders.
   - c. Metaphysical meaning of the four beasts around the throne.
   - d. Metaphysical meaning of the four horsemen.

II.      Readings
   - a. Revelation 4:1-6:8
   - b. *Be Ye Transformed,* Pages 219-226

III.      Questions
   - a. From your own metaphysical understanding, explain the statement, "One seated on the throne."
   - b. List the four beasts and tell what each stands for in human nature.
   - c. What does the book with the seven seals stand for?
   - d. Why is only the Lamb worthy to open the seven seals of the book?
   - e. List the four horsemen and tell what each stands for.

**Introduction and Salutation**

Revelation starts out with the following words:

> [1]*The revelation of Jesus Christ, which God gave him to show his servants what must soon take place; he made it known by sending his angel to his servant John, [2]who testified to the word of God and to the testimony of Jesus Christ, even to all that he saw.*

*3 Blessed is the one who reads aloud the words of the prophecy, and blessed are those who hear and who keep what is written in it; for the time is near.*

*4 John to the seven churches that are in Asia:*

*Grace to you and peace from him who is and who was and who is to come, and from the seven spirits who are before his throne, 5and from Jesus Christ, the faithful witness, the firstborn of the dead, and the ruler of the kings of the earth.*

*To him who loves us and freed us from our sins by his blood, 6and made us to be a kingdom, priests serving his God and Father, to him be glory and dominion for ever and ever. Amen.*

*7Look! He is coming with the clouds; every eye will see him, even those who pierced him; and on his account all the tribes of the earth will wail. So it is to be. Amen.*

*8 'I am the Alpha and the Omega', says the Lord God, who is and who was and who is to come, the Almighty.*

*9 I, John, your brother who share with you in Jesus the persecution and the kingdom and the patient endurance, was on the island called Patmos because of the word of God and the testimony of Jesus. 10I was in the spirit on the Lord's day, and I heard behind me a loud voice like a trumpet 11saying, 'Write in a book what you see and send it to the seven churches, to Ephesus, to Smyrna, to Pergamum, to Thyatira, to Sardis, to Philadelphia, and to Laodicea.'*

*12 Then I turned to see whose voice it was that spoke to me, and on turning I saw seven golden lampstands, 13 and among the lampstands was someone like a son of man,[d] dressed in a robe reaching down to his feet and with a golden sash around his chest. 14 The hair on his head was white like wool, as white as snow, and his eyes were like blazing fire. [15] His feet were like bronze glowing in a furnace, and his voice was like the sound of rushing waters. [16] In his right hand he held seven stars, and coming out of his mouth was a sharp, double-edged sword. His face was like the sun shining in all its brilliance.*

*[17] When I saw him, I fell at his feet as though dead. Then he placed his right hand on me and said: "Do not be afraid. I am the First and the Last. [18] I am the Living One; I was dead, and now look, I am alive for ever and ever! And I hold the keys of death and Hades.*

*[19] "Write, therefore, what you have seen, what is now and what will take place later. [20] The mystery of the seven stars that you saw in my right hand and of the seven golden lampstands is this: The seven stars are the angels[e] of the seven churches, and the seven lampstands are the seven churches.*

The true inspiration of this book is revealed in these opening words. "The Revelation of Jesus Christ, which God gave him to show . . . ." The reality of the presence of Jesus the Christ, and the reality of the Christ Spirit in every person, is the main theme which runs through this book and permeates the whole narrative. The writer states that "God gave him" these revelations, which indicates that the words are, in a sense, being dictated to him directly through the Christ-Mind from universal God-Mind.

Here we have another biblical basis for one of our most frequently used Judeo-Christian affirmations: There is only one presence and one power in the universe and in my life, God, the Good, Omnipotence.

In the Absolute, God is all there really ever was, is now, and ever will be. It is important to realize that this is true for us only in the Absolute. Human beings are related to the Absolute, but we ourselves are not absolutes. Only God is Absolute (unchanging

Omnipresence). People are evolving soul; growing units of universal consciousness with spiritual natures and identities. God is the Infinite; the Absolute.

The author is instructed to write seven letters which will be dictated to him by the Christ. These letters are for seven churches in Asia Minor that were actual churches in early church history, but in *The Revelation* they have a symbolic meaning.

Angels are messengers of light. These messengers are higher thoughts and spiritual energies that come from the higher self, and are received and expressed through the physical vessel.

Since consciousness is a form of light, angels are then messengers of the light of higher consciousness. One of the secrets of Revelation is that the light of higher consciousness comes by the opening of our seven chakras, or spiritual energy portals within our body.

# Chapter 6 - The Message to Ephesus

Ephesus was an ancient Greek city on the coast of Ionia, three kilometers southwest of present-day Selçuk in İzmir Province, Turkey. It was built in the 10th century BC on the site of the former Arzawan capital by Attic and Ionian Greek colonists. During the Classical Greek era it was one of the twelve cities of the Ionian League. The city flourished after it came under the control of the Roman Republic in 129 BCE.

The city was famed for the nearby Temple of Artemis completed around 550 BCE, one of the Seven Wonders of the Ancient World. Among many other monumental buildings are the Library of Celsus, and a theatre capable of holding 25,000 spectators.

Ephesus was one of the seven churches of Asia that are cited in the Book of Revelation. The Gospel of John may have been written here. The city was the site of several 5th century Christian Councils.

The city was destroyed by the Goths in 263CE, and although rebuilt, the city's importance as a commercial center declined as the harbor was slowly silted up by the Küçükmenderes River. It was partially destroyed by an earthquake in 614 CE.

The ruins of Ephesus are a favorite international and local tourist attraction, partly owing to their easy access from Adnan Menderes Airport or from the cruise ship port of Kuşadası, some 30 km to the South.

I.   Major Points
    a.   General metaphysical significance of Revelation in context with the whole Bible.
    b.   God is the ONLY ABSOLUTE. All else is relative and conditional.
    c.   Metaphysical meaning of the church of Ephesus.
    d.   Praise for the church.

       e.   Criticism for the church.

       f.   Promise of reward for overcoming that which is criticized.

II.     Readings

       a.   Revelation 1:1-1:7

       b.   Metaphysical Bible Dictionary: "Ephesus"

       c.   Be Ye Transformed 198-210

III.    Questions

       a.   What is the only Absolute, only Infinite, only Ultimate? Explain.

       b.   Metaphysically, what does the church of Ephesus stand for in human nature?

       c.   Give a general summary of praise given to the church.

       d.   Give a general summary of criticism given to the church.

       e.   Give a general summary of the reward for overcoming to be given.

*2 To the angel of the church in Ephesus write: These are the words of him who holds the seven stars in his right hand, who walks among the seven golden lampstands:*

*3 'I know your works, your toil and your patient endurance. I know that you cannot tolerate evildoers; you have tested those who claim to be apostles but are not, and have found them to be false. 3I also know that you are enduring patiently and bearing up for the sake of my name, and that you have not grown weary.*

*4But I have this against you, that you have abandoned the love you had at first. 5Remember then from what you have fallen; repent, and do the works you did at first. If not, I will come to you and remove your lampstand from its place, unless you repent. 6Yet this is to your credit: you hate the works of the deeds of the Nicolaitans, which I also hate. He who has an ear, let him hear what the Spirit says to the churches. To him who overcomes, I will grant to eat of the tree of life which is in the Paradise of God.*

The seven churches symbolize the seven centers of energy and intelligence within our individuality. They are called "churches" because they constitute factors and processes in our overall spiritual unfoldment. They are components of our method of expressing God. They are all good and very useful, but none are, as yet, perfect. Each has the potential of becoming more perfect.

The name of each church is given at the beginning of each letter. The metaphysical interpretations of those names are all based on the *Metaphysical Bible Dictionary*[61].

The word Ephesus means "desirable; appealing." Metaphysically, it represents our desire nature, and our interpretation of our desire as it pertains to our expression of God. This first of the seven churches represents one of the first things which coming into Truth quickens for us: desire and appeal.

Knowledge of Truth causes a greater desire in us for more knowledge of God and Truth. This growing desire for more of God and His good has become a "church" of worship within our souls, which Revelation names as Ephesus.

Knowledge of Truth has also quickened our awareness of our power of appeal and, consequently, our willingness to ask. We are becoming less reluctant to ask for whatever we deem desirable or useful in our lives. We are less reluctant to ask God on behalf of others. We know the Source, and we are gaining faith in the willingness of that Source to give of its treasures. We are learning to no longer hesitate to appeal to it through prayer, affirmation, and giving thanks in advance. Our church of Ephesus is the symbol of our desire for more of God and more good and,

---

[61] -----*Metaphysical Bible Dictionary* Unity, 2007

also, our willingness to look to God as the omnipresent Source of our good.

Here is the praise for our church of Ephesus. Our desire for good has caused us to become God's workers. This work is inner work. We find we do not become enthused in such work, but are learning to take delight in it. We may not work so much on other things anymore, but rather on our inner thoughts, feelings, and attitudes. We are accomplishing good improvement, and we are becoming less inclined to boast about it.

We are also becoming more patient. Patience is a sure sign of growing spiritual consciousness. Patience is not a self-created accomplishment so much as it is a result, a reward which comes to our soul after making certain inner efforts to become willing to change; to become more conscious of Truth and the good.

"And how you cannot tolerate evildoers" indicates that since we have acknowledged our growing desire for more of God and Truth, we are no longer willing to continue to repeat experiences of useless, unnecessary suffering. The word "*evil*" refers to any attempt to negate any divine idea. Misguided attempts are the cause of suffering. The fact that we no longer want to continue attempts to negate divine ideas or have suffering gives testimony to the growth and improvement we have made in consciousness. We are desiring only Truth and good in our lives and in the lives of others. This is the great accomplishment of the church of Ephesus in us.

A weakness in our desire nature is called to our attention in these words. God is the first love our church of Ephesus responded to. If our desire nature had not made the decision to love God first and foremost, we probably would not have come into the life of Truth. We would have found many other things to do with our lives instead. But we have entered the way; the Truth, and the life revealed to us through Jesus the Christ. This means that our desire nature had to have at some point acknowledged God as our first love. But human desire nature still has the tendency to wander. It becomes fickle. There are yet times when we believe we love other things rather than God. We forget our love for Truth. When this happens, desire can degenerate into covetousness. We become inwardly confused and unhappy. This is because we are not putting our love of God first. Our church of Ephesus has "left its first love.

To "*eat of the tree of life*" means to derive a type of nourishment and some benefit from everything we experience in life, and from all that we observe in life. This is possible for any person who keeps the love of God in first place in his desire nature.

If a person does not really care about Truth, never thinks much about the love of God, is indifferent toward developing spiritual understanding, such a person does not know how to eat of the tree of life. In fact, quite often the opposite happens to him. Life eats her or him! In other words, life experiences and difficulties do not have a nourishing or beneficial effect upon them. Instead, the experiences take a great deal out of them. Those people become easily discouraged, exhausted, and worn out. This is a form of unnecessary suffering. Life should not wear a person out. It should be nourishing and educational; a benefit to the soul. This is exactly how life will become for one who loves God uppermost in her and his desire nature. It is in this way that one gains the secret of eternal nourishment. One learns to extract the good in every life effort, every life experience, literally "*eating of the tree of life.*"

For such a person, what to many people is simply ordinary life, there is a quickening to a new quality of life. That person begins to perceive that their life is really taking place in what the Christ Mind refers to as "*in the paradise of God.*" Paradise is wherever God is, and love of God establishes the Christ Presence within us at all times, under all circumstances.

The church of Ephesus is our Root Chakra. In the message to Ephesus, the message warns us that the higher self has something against the root chakra because in some this chakra is in a state of losing its first love, which is our original spiritual state of union with all that is. In other words, many of us have neglected the spiritual for involvement with the physical life, and therefore the balance between spirituality and physicality has been upset. This unbalance has come about through the development and fortification of our egos and perverted animal desires—yes, even the sexual.

Since we are spiritual beings having a physical experience, our first love is the cultivation and work of the manifestation higher consciousness or the Christ, which is the balance of physical and spiritual life. Unfortunately most of us are caught up in the physical world of the five senses and continually engage in lower thoughts and emotions which strengthen the egos and eventually lead to suffering. This is a complete waste of the potential energy within us.

# Chapter 7 - The Message to Smyrna

Smyrna was an Ancient Greek city located at a central and strategic point on the Aegean coast of Anatolia. This place is known today as İzmir, Turkey. Due to its advantageous port conditions, its ease of defence and its good inland connections, Smyrna rose to prominence. Two sites of the ancient city are today within the boundaries of İzmir. The first site, probably founded by indigenous peoples, rose to prominence during the Archaic Period as one of the principal ancient Greek settlements in western Anatolia. The second, whose foundation is associated with Alexander the Great, reached metropolitan proportions during the period of the Roman Empire. Most of the present-day remains of the ancient city date from the Roman era, the majority from after a 2nd-century CE earthquake.

In practical terms, a distinction is often made between these. Old Smyrna was the initial settlement founded around the 11th century BCE, first as an Aeolian settlement, and later taken over and developed during the Archaic Period by the Ionians. Smyrna proper was the new city which residents moved to as of the 4th century BCE and whose foundation was inspired by Alexander the Great.

Old Smyrna was located on a small peninsula connected to the mainland by a narrow isthmus at the northeastern corner of the inner Gulf of İzmir, at the edge of a fertile plain and at the foot of Mount Yamanlar. This Anatolian settlement commanded the gulf. Today, the archeological site, named Bayraklı Höyüğü, is approximately 700 metres (770 yd) inland, in the Tepekule neighbourhood of Bayraklı.

The core of the late Hellenistic and early Roman Smyrna is preserved in the large area of İzmir Agora Open Air Museum at this site. Research is being pursued at the sites of both the old and the new cities. This has been conducted since 1997 for Old Smyrna and since 2002 for the Classical Period city, in collaboration between the İzmir Archaeology Museum and the Metropolitan Municipality of İzmir.

I. Major Points
  a. Metaphysical meaning of the church of Smyrna.
  b. Praise for the church.
  c. Criticism for the church.
  d. Promise of reward for overcoming that which is criticized.
II. Readings
  a. Revelation 2:7-2:11
  b. Metaphysical Bible Dictionary: "Smyrna"
  c. Be Ye Transformed Page 210
III. Questions
  a. Metaphysically, what does the church of Smyrna stand for in human nature?
  b. Give a general summary of praise given to the church.
  c. Give a general summary of criticism given to the church.
  d. Give a general summary of the reward for overcoming to be given.

`        [8] And to the angel of the church in Smyrna write: These are the words of the first and the last, who was dead and came to life:*
[9] 'I know your affliction and your poverty, even though you are rich. I know the slander on the part of those who say that they are Jews and are not, but are a synagogue of Satan. [10]Do not fear what you are about to suffer. Beware, the devil is about to throw some of you into prison so that you may be tested, and for ten days you will have affliction. Be faithful until death, and I will give you the crown of life. [11]Let anyone who has an ear*

*listen to what the Spirit is saying to the churches.*
*Whoever conquers will not be harmed by the second*
*death.*

The word Smyrna means "flowing; distilling; spiritous." Metaphysically, Smyrna stands for spiritual substance. The church of Smyrna symbolizes a person's consciousness of substance.

What is substance? The word is used differently in Unity from the way it is used in conventional science. In science, the word pertains to matter. In Unity, the word refers to spiritual energy which is not material, but is the basis for all possibilities of material form. Substance is the basis for supply and prosperity, and a consciousness of substance generates true prosperity for a person.

The definition of the word Smyrna ("flowing; distilling; spiritous") actually somewhat describes the nature of substance. In a sense, it is "flowing" all about us and within us at all times. It is the invisible, intangible reality of energy, containing all potential of form. It is not material but is the essence out of which all material is "distilled."

Charles Fillmore taught that substance responds to man's thought of it. Man's consciousness causes substance to produce effects from itself into the realm which man experiences as three-dimensional form. These forms are then used by us and become our supply and our prosperity.

In its primary state, substance is spiritual, and it is pure and "good." It is also unlimited and omnipresent. It responds to any human being who is willing to become aware of it and who thinks about it in the right way.[62]

*I know your tribulation and your poverty (but you are rich)*
*...*

---

[62] 2:9

Every human being is completely rich as far as substance is concerned. Whether or not a person realizes it, his very existence is immersed in the substance of God's good, and is permeated by it. Lack, poverty, or failure in a person's life are the effects of ignorance, indifference, or unbelief toward spiritual substance. The person may not in any way be guilty of any wrongdoing in this respect, but spiritual substance can only await his awakening before it can flow through his consciousness and enrich his life.

The Christ Mind knows the struggle of the human mind in the face of lack or poverty. It says, "I know your tribulation and your poverty." But it immediately adds these words, "but you are rich." This means that whatever our past experience of lack may have been, and whatever current challenge we may be facing of a poverty nature, a prosperity consciousness can, and will, be quickened in us if we will take the right steps. We can do this by activating the church of Smyrna within us by giving our belief and willingness to the divine idea of God's spiritual substance within us and all around us at all times.

What is a prosperity consciousness? Primarily it is something developed in the mind of a person who has learned to depend on God as his true source of supply. We must have faith in God as Creator and Source of all good. When we do, spiritual substance will see to it that forms of good are always available in abundance to us. Our consciousness has the power to cause a "flowing" and "distilling" process to occur in the very substance of our lives, and the result is that we have all sufficiency in all things, with much to spare and to share. This is the true prosperity consciousness, symbolized as the church of Smyrna.[63]

> I know ... the slander of those who say that they are Jews
> and are not, but are a synagogue of Satan.

---

[63] 2:9

"Jews" stand for thoughts and feelings turned toward spiritual Truth. "Satan" stands for erroneous thoughts and negative emotions.[64] The highly symbolic words in verse nine pertain to some of the false beliefs and negative attitudes which are still active in our thinking about prosperity. Some of these false beliefs may outwardly appear to be helpful to our progress in prosperity consciousness (they say they are Jews) but are actually harmful to our prosperity consciousness (and are not, but are of the synagogue of Satan). These erroneous beliefs may wear some clever disguises and be deceiving many persons, but knowledge of Truth reveals them to be errors, and they must be cast out of our prosperity thinking. Some examples of them are:

It is possible for me to get my good at another's expense.

There is the danger that another might get his good at my expense.

The only way to experience prosperity is to possess many things, and the more things, the better.

If a certain channel of supply in life is taken away, that means that a person's source of good has been taken away.

One must never give more than he can expect to get back quickly in return.[65]

*He who has an ear, let him hear what the Spirit says to the churches. He who conquers shall not be hurt by the second death.*

How do we overcome false beliefs which promise us much but which really only spoil our prosperity consciousness? We can begin by making the effort to base all our thinking about prosperity on the divine idea of substance. God's substance is for

---

[64] See Yeaw, James *Perception* CreateSpace, 2007 Translation of Satan is *Accuser*
[65] 2:11

everyone. Next, rely on God, trust in God. Speak words of thanksgiving for the prospering power of God's substance in our lives. Give thanks that all the ideas in Divine Mind are ours to receive and use and share. These ideas will then go to work for us and cause to come forth that which will constitute our rightful supply and prosperity.

We should always remember that the most powerful action we can take as human beings as far as prosperity is concerned is to cooperate with the great law of giving and receiving. Giving is so very, very important where true prosperity is concerned. Share generously. Pay bills cheerfully. Accept gifts happily. Be grateful for bargains, enjoy finding them, but treat the business of bargaining very lightly.

Then there is the matter of borrowing and lending. These, too, come under the law governing prosperity. If we loan to another person, we should do so with the feeling that we were giving him something. This does not mean that we do not allow him to pay us back. But it does have to do with our attitude about loaning. If we are the borrower, then we should make the effort to put ourselves in the place of the one from whom we borrow. This keeps borrowing and lending squarely within the laws of spiritual prosperity, and all will be well.

The final words of the letter to the church of Smyrna are, "'He who conquers shall not be hurt by the second death.'"

Metaphysically, the "first death" refers to something leaving a past form of existence prior to assuming its next form of existence. "Second death" refers to when something leaves its current form of existence prior to assuming its future form of existence.

For example, when a baby is born, that soul has, in a sense, "died" to the state of existence it was in before it assumed its place in physical birth. From our perspective, its "first death" was to its prenatal state.

The life form of an acorn "dies" to its acorn existence in order to proceed into its oak tree form of existence. If some fine furniture is to be made out of that oak wood, then the life form of "oak tree" will "die" in order to proceed into the fine furniture form of its existence.

The word "death", as often used in the Bible, does not mean cessation of life but, rather, a change in the state of existence of certain life forms. In earthly life, this is occurring all the time. Forms come, forms change, forms go, new forms are evolved. The problem for many human beings is that many of us are still being "hurt" by the "second death" of a number of things.

The promise in this letter is "'He who conquers shall not be hurt by the second death.'" This means that when we are established in a true prosperity consciousness, based upon spiritual understanding of God's laws and God's substance, the comings and goings of outer forms of things will no longer hurt us. We do not feel damaged or cheated when certain forms of things change or are removed. When we really understand that God's spiritual substance fills every part of our lives, every moment of our lives, then we never feel separated from the true Source of our good.

The church of Smyrna represents this chakra. Whereas the first chakra is connected with our sexual organs where the potential for physical creation resides, this chakra is associated with sexual function and the process of procreation. The message states that the works are known: *thy works, and tribulation, and poverty* because this is where situations can seem desperate when we are seeking to transmute sexual energy into spiritual energy. In reality, this church is rich because the energy associated with this chakra is truly great, but we experience tribulation and poverty when we begin denial of the ego and the physical pleasures of life in order to gain spiritual benefit. When we restrain our basic animal instincts, many hormones begin to balance in the body; especially our fight or flight hormones and we can even take control of fear. We symbolically conquer death when we conqueror our fears.

# Chapter 8 - The Message to Pergamum

Pergamon was a rich and powerful ancient Greek city in Aeolis. It is located 26 kilometres (16 mi) from the modern coastline of the Aegean Sea on a promontory on the north side of the river Caicus and northwest of the modern city of Bergama.

Many remains of its impressive monuments can still be seen and especially the outstanding masterpiece of the Pergamon Altar.

It became the capital of the Kingdom of Pergamon during the Hellenistic period under the Attalid dynasty in 281–133 BCE.

Pergamon is cited in the Book of Revelation as one of the seven churches of Asia.

I.   Major Points
   a.  Metaphysical meaning of the church of Pergamum.
   b.  Praise for the church.
   c.  Criticism for the church.
   d.  Promise of reward for overcoming that which is criticized.
II.  Readings
   a.  Revelation 2:12-2:17
   b.  Metaphysical Bible Dictionary: "Pergamum-"
   c.  Be Ye Transformed 211, 212
III. Questions
   a.  Metaphysically, what does the church of Pergamum stand for in human nature?
   b.  Give a general summary of praise given to the church.
   c.  Give a general summary of criticism given to the church.
   d.  Give a general summary of the reward for overcoming to be given

*¹² And to the angel of the church in Pergamum write: These are the words of him who has the sharp two-edged sword:*

*¹³ 'I know where you are living, where Satan's throne is. Yet you are holding fast to my name, and you did not deny your faith in me even in the days of Antipas my witness, my faithful one, who was killed among you, where Satan lives. ¹⁴But I have a few things against you: you have some there who hold to the teaching of Balaam, who taught Balak to put a stumbling-block before the people of Israel, so that they would eat food sacrificed to idols and practise fornication. ¹⁵So you also have some who hold to the teaching of the Nicolaitans. ¹⁶Repent then. If not, I will come to you soon and make war against them with the sword of my mouth. ¹⁷Let anyone who has an ear listen to what the Spirit is saying to the churches. To everyone who conquers I will give some of the hidden manna, and I will give a white stone, and on the white stone is written a new name that no one knows except the one who receives it.*

Pergamum means "strongly united; closely knit." *The Metaphysical Bible Dictionary*[66] gives the metaphysical meaning of the church of Pergamum as "intellectual nature." More specifically, it stands for the cooperation of our intellect in the whole process of spiritual unfoldment.[67]

> *I know where you dwell, where Satan's throne is; you hold fast my name and you did not deny my faith. ...*

This is praise given to our intellect. Our intellect is "holding fast" to our commitment to Spirit even though "Satan's throne" is

---

[66] ---*Metaphysical Bible Dictionary*, Unity Books, 2007
[67] 2:13

located within it. Satan is the biblical symbol of negative thinking and erroneous beliefs. Satan's throne represents that matrix for all human error and negativity. It is located in the human intellect. The Christ Mind praises our intellect for "holding fast" in spite of the fact that so much negativity and error are going on within it!

When we consider that "Satan's throne" is right within our intellect at this time, we cannot help but wonder how we have managed to keep ourselves as faithful and loyal to Truth as we have.

But praiseworthy as it is, our intellect is in need of further improvement when it comes to cooperating with the process of spiritual unfoldment.[68]

> But I have a few things against you: you have some there who hold the teaching of Balaam... eat food sacrificed to idols and practice immorality.

These things mentioned are symbolic references to very common faults and shortcomings still active in the intellects of human beings who are otherwise committed to Spirit and to Truth. It is not necessary to be too specific about what these errors actually are, but in general they are:

- Superstitious and negative types of religious thinking.
- Materialistic greed and worship of personalities.
- Connecting our sense of I Am to negative emotions.

> He who has an ear, let him hear what the Spirit says to the churches. To him who conquers I will give some of the hidden manna, and I will give him a white stone, with a new name written on the stone which no one knows except him who receives it.[69]

---

[68] 2:14
[69] 2:17

First, how do we overcome and correct the faults and shortcomings in our intellectual nature where spiritual unfoldment is concerned? Nothing is more helpful than the Unity method of correct use of denial and affirmation. The intellect is thus being trained to "feed" on divine ideas instead of "food sacrificed to idols." This also trains our intellect to connect our sense of I AM only to divine ideas instead of erroneous beliefs and negative emotions. Charles Fillmore taught that the correct use of denial and affirmation would eventually "spiritualize the whole intellect."

The first part of the reward promised for this particular overcoming is: "I will give some of the hidden manna." - This refers to the discovery of an entirely new source of energy and nourishment. This source is not a visible, tangible "something" out in the world. It is a "hidden" source, which means that it is within. It is simply the higher levels of our own being.

The nourishment derived from these higher levels of being within us is more than physical. It nourishes the soul first, then the body. It benefits the whole man. There is no waste matter; nothing needs to be eliminated following its assimilation by us. In the Gospels, Jesus alludes to this very thing when He says to His disciples,[70] "I have food to eat of which you do not know." This "hidden manna" is the vital life, substance, and energy of Spirit, directly assimilated into our entire being. Other symbolic terms that refer to this are "bread from heaven," "body of Christ," "blood of Christ."

The second part of the reward promised is, "'... and I will give him a white stone, with a new name written on the stone which no one knows except him who receives it.'" This refers to a new and higher realization of I AM. In the past, when most of us said, "I am," we were usually thinking of only our current opinions

---

[70] John 4:32

of ourselves. Greater realization of I AM is much more than an opinion of one's self, it is more of an awareness of our Real Self. Our Real Self is so much greater than any opinion we can ever have of ourself. It requires our reaching a higher level of consciousness within ourselves to even bear facing a realization of our Real Self. This is the "white stone" mentioned. In this "white stone," or purified state of consciousness, we learn our "new name," an entirely new realization of our true I AM.

Pergamos is the third chakra, or solar plexus. It is quite powerful, either for positive spiritual transformation or continually fortifying the ego. Negative energy from this chakra can manifest in the form of anger and impulsive reactions which kill spiritual aspirations. Jesus states that this is Satan's seat because the solar plexus is responsible for emotional desires and impulses. In other words, our astral body or emotional body works through our solar plexus.

This center is also connected with the intellect. Thus it is our spiritual job to stay away from eating things sacrificed to idols—i.e., anything that gets us caught up in our lower thoughts and emotions such as judgment and pride.

*Gaskell's Dictionary of Scripture and Myth*[71] defines idols as:

> *A symbol of conventional mental conceptions; mistaken notions of the object of life; fixed ideas which bar the way to Truth; outward observances regarded as ethical or spiritual exercises; unworthy objects of life.*

Thus even getting caught up in church doctrines can seriously entrench our egos and cause us to be judgmental to everyone who disagrees with us. Committing fornication is to lie with our negative emotions and desires by feeding them through

---

[71] Gaskell, G. A. *Gaskell's Dictionary of Scripture and* Julian Press, 1976

the Satan (ego) within. This is also the practice of the Nicoliatans, which is hated.

# Chapter 9 - The Message to Thyateira

Thyateira was the name of an ancient Greek city in Asia Minor, now the modern Turkish city of Akhisar ("white castle"). It lies in the far west of Turkey, south of Istanbul and almost due east of Athens. It is about 50 miles (80 km) from the Aegean Sea.

I.  Major Points
   a. Metaphysical meaning of the church of Thyateira.
   b. Praise for the church.
   c. Criticism for the church.
   d. Promise of reward for overcoming that which is criticized.
II.  Readings
   a. Revelation 2:18-2:29
   b. Metaphysical Bible Dictionary: "Thyatira"
   c. Be Ye Transformed 212, 213
III.  Questions
   a. Metaphysically, what does the church of Thyateira stand for in human nature?
   b. Give a general summary of praise given to the church.
   c. Give a general summary of criticism given to the church.
   d. Give a general summary of the reward for overcoming to be given.

$^{18}$ *And to the angel of the church in Thyatira write: These are the words of the Son of God, who has eyes like a flame of fire, and whose feet are like burnished bronze:*
$^{19}$ *'I know your works—your love, faith, service, and patient endurance. I know that your last works are greater than the first.* $^{20}$*But I have this against you: you tolerate that woman Jezebel, who calls herself a prophet and is*

*teaching and beguiling my servants to practice fornication
and to eat food sacrificed to idols. $^{21}$I gave her time to
repent, but she refuses to repent of her fornication.
$^{22}$Beware, I am throwing her on a bed, and those who
commit adultery with her I am throwing into great distress,
unless they repent of her doings; $^{23}$and I will strike her
children dead. And all the churches will know that I am the
one who searches minds and hearts, and I will give to each
of you as your works deserve. $^{24}$But to the rest of you in
Thyatira, who do not hold this teaching, who have not
learned what some call "the deep things of Satan", to you I
say, I do not lay on you any other burden; $^{25}$only hold fast
to what you have until I come. $^{26}$To everyone who conquers
and continues to do my works to the end,I will give
authority over the nations; $^{27}$to rule them with an iron
rod, as when clay pots are shattered— $^{28}$even as I also
received authority from my Father. To the one who
conquers I will also give the morning star. $^{29}$Let anyone
who has an ear listen to what the Spirit is saying to the
churches.*

Thyateira means "rushing headlong; burning incense." *The
Metaphysical Bible Dictionary*[72] gives the metaphysical meaning of
this church as: "Zeal is the central thought represented by this
church; it is also connected with power and faith." We can think
of the church of Thyateira as the zeal center within us in
connection with our spiritual unfoldment. Zeal is the quality which
makes us enthusiastic and interested in all that aids our growth in
consciousness. It enables us to remain enthusiastic and interested
in life itself. Without it we would be entirely passive, subjective,

---

[72] ----- *Metaphysical Bible Dictionary*, Unity, 2007, p. 654

and mechanical. With it we are always able to be motivated and inspired.[73]

> "'I know your works, your love and faith and service and patient endurance, and that your latter works exceed the first.'"

We notice that in the wording of this praise, the first thing mentioned is "works," and the last thing mentioned is also "works," followed by, "and that your latter works exceed the first." In other words, progressively greater works. This is true progress. Zeal is the quality most involved in gaining progress. If the zeal center (church of Thyatira) was not active in us, our lives would be in danger of becoming treadmills of tedious and pointless activity. Spiritual unfoldment would be impeded seriously. But zeal prevents this from happening.[74]

But I have this against you, that you tolerate the woman Jezebel ...

The word Jezebel means, among other things, "licentious; adulterous; uncontrolled." Metaphysically she stands for negative emotions. Negative emotions can be very hard to control but unless they are, they can do great damage. As an actual character, Jezebel was evidently a seductive but extremely dangerous person. Metaphysically this also seems true about what she symbolizes. Few persons can resist their allure. But to succumb to them always brings painful results.

Why is there something so strangely attractive to us in negative emotions? Possibly one reason is that they always promise us the pleasure of a kind of excitement. We are attracted to excitement, even negative excitement. But negative

---

[73] 2:19
[74] 2:20

excitement is so often followed by depression. That is often the penalty for succumbing to Jezebel (negative emotions).[75]

> *Behold, I will throw her on a sickbed, and those who commit adultery with her I will throw into great tribulation, unless they repent of her doings.*

The type of adultery mentioned here consists of connecting our sense of I AM to any negative emotions. Negative emotions come into all persons at various times. But no great harm is done if they simply come to a person. But great harm will be done if a person places his sense of I AM into them. This is the "sin" of adultery. To "repent of this sin" simply means to disconnect your sense of I AM from whatever negative emotion it had been connected to. Once we begin to seriously practice refusing to connect our sense of I AM to any negative emotions that come to us, we are on the way to perfect self-control and spiritual dominion and mastery.[76]

> *He who conquers and who keeps my works until the end, I will give him power over the nations, and he shall rule them with a rod of iron ... and I will give him the morning star.*

This reward symbolizes perfect self-control; non-negative self discipline. There is no guilt or regret connected with this kind of self-control and discipline. The "morning star" is a symbol of divine guidance. Divine guidance being followed with zeal, self-control, and self-discipline helps us to become what we are designed to become: masters of existence!

---

[75] 2:22
[76] 2:26-28

Thyatira is the heart chakra. Notice how the message states that the work of charity, service, patience, and faith is known. These are the works of the heart. Through this chakra we learn to bridge the gap between ourselves and our community. This is the last chakra of the lower temple, and therefore it should extend beyond us and to the community. Love is a divine power of God because it links us with the collective. But as is stated, Jezebel easily takes hold here. Jezebel was responsible for taking the heart of the people away from serving God. It is in effect living a life of physical pursuit without any spiritual aspirations. This can cause us to become dispassionate about life in general and it slowly zaps the spiritual desire from our lives.

When the heart chakra, the last gate of the lower temple, is opened, the stage is set for the next three chakras of the higher temple to bring higher consciousness to the individual.

# Chapter 10 – The Message to Sardis

Sardis was an ancient city at the location of modern Sart in Turkey's Manisa Province. Sardis was the capital of the ancient kingdom of Lydia, one of the important cities of the Persian Empire, the seat of a proconsul under the Roman Empire, and the metropolis of the province Lydia in later Roman and Byzantine times. As one of the seven churches of Asia, it was addressed by John, the author of the Book of Revelation, in terms which seem to imply that its population was notoriously soft and fainthearted. Its importance was due first to its military strength, secondly to its situation on an important highway leading from the interior to the Aegean coast, and thirdly to its commanding the wide and fertile plain of the Hermus.

I.     Major Points
   a. Metaphysical meaning of the church of Sardis.
   b. Praise for the church.
   c. Criticism for the church.
   d. Promise of reward for overcoming that which is criticized.
II.    Readings
   a. Revelation 3:1-3:6
   b. Metaphysical Bible Dictionary: "Sardis"
   c. Be Ye Transformed 213-215
III.   Questions
   a. Metaphysically, what does the church of Sardis stand for in human nature?
   b. Give a general summary of praise given to the church.
   c. Give a general summary of criticism given to the church.
   d. Give a general summary of the reward for overcoming to be given.

*"To the angel of the church in Sardis write:*

*These are the words of him who holds the seven spirits[b] of God and the seven stars. I know your deeds; you have a reputation of being alive, but you are dead. ² Wake up! Strengthen what remains and is about to die, for I have found your deeds unfinished in the sight of my God. ³ Remember, therefore, what you have received and heard; hold it fast, and repent. But if you do not wake up, I will come like a thief, and you will not know at what time I will come to you.*

*⁴ Yet you have a few people in Sardis who have not soiled their clothes. They will walk with me, dressed in white, for they are worthy. ⁵ The one who is victorious will, like them, be dressed in white. I will never blot out the name of that person from the book of life, but will acknowledge that name before my Father and his angels. ⁶ Whoever has ears, let them hear what the Spirit says to the churches.*

The word Sardis means "precious gem; prince of joy." Metaphysically, it stands for our inner center of joyous power and dominion; our true awareness of our spiritual individuality.

I know your works; you have the name of being alive, and you are dead. Awake, and strengthen what remains and is on the point of death, for I have not found your works perfect in the sight of my God.[77]

These are very strange words, mixing praise and criticism within one statement. They indicate and the Christ Mind judges that we have been using our individual power and dominion in an

---

[77] 3:1,2

only slightly satisfactory way. It is a church in us that is alive and, yet, is also "dead." This is a paradox but, nevertheless, it is true.

We have been taught since we came into Truth that, as children of God, we have spiritual power, dominion, and authority as individuals. Jesus told us that the same power that was in Him is also in us and that we should follow Him in using that power as we see the need for it. We are free to follow Divine Guidance in expressing our individuality. And we have done so. But to what degree? This letter indicates that it has been to very little degree. It indicates that our individual power and dominion is remaining dormant for the most part. This inference is contained in the words, "and you are dead."

What can be causing this? What factors may be holding back our full expression of the power and dominion that is ours? There appear to be at least two possible reasons:

(1) Many of us have the tendency to wait to use our spiritual power until some very big issue comes up in our lives. There is the tendency to think that spiritual power should only be called forth to handle great, important problems or events. But if we wait for the big, big challenges to come up before we exercise our spiritual power and dominion, we may have too long to wait. Stagnation and inertia may set in, and we will become weak.

The solution? We can use our spiritual power and dominion in the so-called little things of life. Everyday problems, common troubles, any healing need we become aware of, ordinary misunderstandings, in fact, all the little details of life are valid opportunities for us to call forth and use our individual power and dominion.

(2) The second reason why our inner spiritual power may seem to become depleted (go dead) is that we tend to externalize too much of it when we do use it. That is, we sometimes become more concerned with outer accomplishments than we are in inner soul growth. The wisest and most productive use of our power and dominion is on our inner self, our own thinking, emotions,

attitudes, reactions. Power used here causes an increase of power, not a depletion.

> *He who conquers shall be clad thus in white garments, and I will not blot his name out of the book of life; I will confess his name before my Father and before his angels.*[78]

The first part of this promise mentions the reward of being "clad thus in white garments." "White garments" is a symbol of two things: .clean feeling about one's self, and a pure, non-negative attitude connected with self-control. This type of self-control is not the grim and determined type of negative self-control. Rather it is a matter of thinking, feeling, and doing only what your Real Self knows to be best. The motive is desire for the highest good of all. This type of self-control gives us a truly "clean" feeling (white garments).

The second part of the promise is, "'I will not blot his name out of the book of life; I will confess his name before my Father and before his angels, To be "blotted out of the book of life" means to have a feeling of being useless in God's world. It is also a feeling of suffering a loss of individuality.

When we overcome these negative feelings by affirming the Truth of our oneness with the Father, our sense of individuality is restored, and the false belief in our uselessness is eliminated. Instead of thinking of ourselves as "blots" in the book of life, we know that our "names" are fully written out in the book of life.

Earlier, in the Gospels, Jesus states this same idea when He says to the returning seventy, "... rejoice that your names are written in heaven." [79] Your name written in heaven refers to knowing your true identity and your right place within life.

---

[78] 3:5
[79] Luke 10:20

This church of Sardis relate to the throat chakra. Traditionally, this chakra has been associated with hearing and speech. Most of us experience life relatively unconsciously, so whatever we put into the human conscious experience will be regurgitated, particularly through speech. What we say comes from the heart. Our speech says a lot about what we have become and who we are. It is interesting that this chakra is associated with the thyroid gland which produces hormones responsible for growth and maturation. Therefore as energy moves up the spine through the region of the neck and throat, we mature spiritually through the purification in our thoughts, actions, and speech.

Make note of the fact that "name" in Revelations 3:1 refers to *authority* or *character*. It's a derivative of the Greek word which means *"be aware, known, perceive, speak, and understand."*

This is about the authority and character of our entire being, which is contained in right speech and action. Our speech comes from the heart and entirety of who we are. Proverbs tells us that the power of life and death is in the tongue. That's why it's so important to both think and speak life. The message tells us that in order to strengthen what is within, it must be purified by death. This is the death of our character in exchange for higher consciousness. This will produce right action, and right speech, which is associated with the color white. The message states:[80]

*He that overcomes, the same shall be clothed in white rainment...*

---

[80] 3:5

# Chapter 11 – The Message to Philadelphia

Alaşehir, in Antiquity and the Middle Ages known as Philadelphia is a town and district of Manisa Province in the Aegean region of Turkey. It is situated in the valley of the Kuzuçay (Cogamus in antiquity), at the foot of the Bozdağ Mountain.

It stands on elevated ground commanding the extensive and fertile plain of the Gediz River, presents at a distance an imposing appearance. It has 45 mosques . There are small industries and a fair trade. From one of the mineral springs comes a heavily charged water popular around Turkey.

Within Turkey, the city's name is synonymous with the dried Sultana raisins, although cultivation for the fresh fruit market, less labor-intensive than the dried fruit, gained prominence in the last decades. As Philadelphia, Alaşehir was a highly important center in the Early Christian and Byzantine periods. Today it remains a strong center of Orthodox Christianity, and remains a titular see of the Roman Catholic Church.

I.   Major Points
   a.   Metaphysical meaning of the church of Philadelphia.
   b.   Praise for the church.
   c.   Criticism for the church.
   d.   Promise of reward for overcoming that which is criticized.
II.  Readings
   a.   Revelation 3:7-3:13
   b.   Metaphysical Bible Dictionary: "Philadelphia"
   c.   Be Ye Transformed 215, 216
III. Questions

a. Metaphysically, what does the church of Philadelphia stand for in human nature?
b. Give a general summary of praise given to the church.
c. Give a general summary of criticism given to the church.
d. Give a general summary of the reward for overcoming to be given.

$^7$ *"To the angel of the church in Philadelphia write:*
*These are the words of him who is holy and true, who holds the key of David. What he opens no one can shut, and what he shuts no one can open. 8 I know your deeds. See, I have placed before you an open door that no one can shut. I know that you have little strength, yet you have kept my word and have not denied my name. 9 I will make those who are of the synagogue of Satan, who claim to be Jews though they are not, but are liars—I will make them come and fall down at your feet and acknowledge that I have loved you. 10 Since you have kept my command to endure patiently, I will also keep you from the hour of trial that is going to come on the whole world to test the inhabitants of the earth.*

$^{11}$ *I am coming soon. Hold on to what you have, so that no one will take your crown. 12 The one who is victorious I will make a pillar in the temple of my God. Never again will they leave it. I will write on them the name of my God and the name of the city of my God, the new Jerusalem, which is coming down out of heaven from my God; and I will also write on them my new name.*
*13 Whoever has ears, let them hear what the Spirit says to the churches.*

The word Philadelphia means "brotherly love." Metaphysically, it is the center of the human expression of love. As a divine idea, there is only one love. The church of Philadelphia does not stand for the divine idea of love, but for the many modes of human expression of love. In human nature, the current realization and expression of love as commonly practiced is quite limited and imperfect (in comparison to what it might be). For this reason, very little praise for this church is contained in this letter. It simply states: "'I know your works.'"[81]

But this abrupt statement is immediately followed by words of wonderful reassurance: "'... I have set before you an open door, which no one is able to shut; I know that you have but little power, and yet you have kept my word and have not denied my name.'"[82]

These words tell us something about our human love nature which we are glad to hear. Even though most human beings are not at present accomplishing things through love which could and should be accomplished, nevertheless, a genuine desire to do so is present in most persons. The Christ Mind recognizes this. Most people want to be more loving. Most people have good intentions about giving and receiving love in right ways. Most people would rather be kind than unkind. No one seems to be perfect in any of this as yet. But we want to be! And that is what counts in Spirit. So the Christ Mind has made this wonderful provision for us: "'Behold, I have set before you an open door, which no one is able to shut. ...'"

What this means is the Christ Power has established eternal opportunity for our human love nature. Never will we be deprived of love in our lives. We need not fear that we will be deprived of opportunities to give and receive love. We need never worry that the time will come when we will not be loved or will not have

---

[81] 3:8
[82] 3:8

anyone to love. This shall not happen. This is a promise of the Christ Mind. It has decreed to our human love nature (church of Philadelphia) that one open door has been set before it (eternal opportunities to love) and that nothing in the outer can take this away from it (no one can shut it).

There is a lovely affirmation one may use to help keep this realization alive in consciousness:

> *I am a radiating center of divine love: mighty to attract my good and radiate good to others.*

But like most aspects of human nature at its present level of development, there is a shortcoming. In our human love nature, this shortcoming is pointed out in words very similar to those found in the letter to the church in Smyrna.[83]

> *Behold, I will make those of the synagogue of Satan who say that they are Jews and are not, but lie...*

Once again, as in the case of the church of Smyrna (prosperity thinking), we have the danger of the presence of thoughts, feelings, beliefs, and attitudes which claim to be helping the development of our love nature (they say they are Jews) but are actually hindering the correct expression of our love nature (are not Jews, but are of the synagogue of Satan).

It is a sad fact that although humanity values love very highly, considering it the most beautiful of all spiritual qualities, there are still many mistaken beliefs, attitudes, and actions in regard to expressing it, especially in the give-and-take among human beings. Some of these errors have become so widely accepted that it becomes difficult to change them. But once they are detected as errors in our thinking, change is then very possible. Among them we might list:

---

[83] 3:9

In a human love relationship, it is necessary to have certain negative emotions, such as possessiveness, passion, jealousy, and exaggerated sentimentality.

The belief that someone or something can take love away from us.

The notion that love is something which can only come to us from without. This is a reversal of Truth, and it causes many wrong connections and wrong priorities in our thinking. Love can be experienced by us as we radiate it from within.

The belief that we should evaluate the love that is in our lives by comparing it with the love which seems to be in other persons' lives. The Truth is that love should be felt as an individual precious thing, with no need to make comparisons with what another has.

The tendency to love only those who first give us pleasure or who serve our self interests.[84] [85]

> Him who conquers, I will make him a pillar in the temple of my God; never shall he go out of it, and I will write on him the name of my God, and the name of the city of my God, the new Jerusalem which comes from my God out of heaven, and my own new name.

This promise symbolically describes the attainment of a state of true inner peace, poise, and stability. This most satisfying of all possible inner states is gained by overcoming most of the erroneous beliefs and attitudes concerning human love and following a more spiritually correct pattern in expressing human love.

---

[84] Jesus had some interesting things to say about this. Read Matt. 5:43-48.
[85] 3:12

"I will make him a pillar in the temple of my God" symbolizes the attainment of a realization of strength and peace (pillar).

"Never shall he go out of it" symbolizes becoming no longer a creature of emotional moods, whims, and one who is prone to "fall out" of love without warning.

"I will write on him the name of my God" refers to the name of the human concept of God, which is I AM. (I AM is not really the name of God, but rather names the human concept of or human perception of God.)

"'... and the name of the city of my God, the new Jerusalem...'" The word Jerusalem means "habitation of peace." To have the name of God (I AM) and the name of the city of my God (habitation of peace) written upon a person, symbolizes the gaining by that person of a new realization that: I am the habitation of God's peace and my heart is the abode of God's perfect love.

The church of Philadelphia pertains to the 6th chakra. Of this church, the message states:[86]

> *"And to the angel in the church of Philadelphia write; These things saith he that is holy, he that is true, he that hath the key of David, he that openeth, and no man shutteth, and shutteth and no man openeth; I know they works: behold, I have set before thee and open door, and no man can shut it: for thou hast a little strength, and has kept my word, and no denied my name. Because thou has kept the word of my patience, I will keep thee from the hour of temptation...Him that overcometh will I make a pillar in the temple of my God..."*

---

[86] 3:7-11

The sixth chakra is traditionally associated with wisdom and the seat of the mind. This door that is opened is the beginning to higher consciousness and the establishment of one as a pillar in the house of God. Learning patience through meditation and living in the now is crucial to opening this chakra. We walk through the door that Jesus has opened here through these two methods of action. By living these actions, we continue to keep the word of his patience and will eventually overcome so that we may be established as a pillar in the house of God.

# Chapter 12 – The Message to Laodicea

Laodicea on the Lycus was an ancient city built on the river Lycus (Çürüksu). It was located in the Hellenistic regions of Caria and Lydia, which later became the Roman Province of Phrygia Pacatiana. It is now situated near the modern city of Denizli.

It contained one of the Seven churches of Asia mentioned in the Book of Revelation.

I.     Major Points
    a. Metaphysical meaning of the church of Laodicea.
    b. Praise for the church.
    c. Criticism for the church.
    d. Promise of reward for overcoming that which is criticized.
II.    Readings
    a. Revelation 3:14-3:22
    b. Metaphysical Bible Dictionary: "Laodicea"
    c. Be Ye Transformed 217, 218
III.   Questions
    a. Metaphysically, what does the church of Laodicea stand for in human nature?
    b. Give a general summary of praise given to the church.
    c. Give a general summary of criticism given to the church.
    d. Give a general summary of the reward for overcoming to be given.

*14 "To the angel of the church in Laodicea write: These are the words of the Amen, the faithful and true witness, the ruler of God's creation. 15 I know your deeds, that you are neither cold nor hot. I wish you were*

*either one or the other! 16 So, because you are*
*lukewarm—neither hot nor cold—I am about to spit you*
*out of my mouth. 17 You say, 'I am rich; I have acquired*
*wealth and do not need a thing.' But you do not realize*
*that you are wretched, pitiful, poor, blind and naked. 18 I*
*counsel you to buy from me gold refined in the fire, so you*
*can become rich; and white clothes to wear, so you can*
*cover your shameful nakedness; and salve to put on your*
*eyes, so you can see.*

*19 Those whom I love I rebuke and discipline. So be*
*earnest and repent. 20 Here I am! I stand at the door and*
*knock. If anyone hears my voice and opens the door, I will*
*come in and eat with that person, and they with me.*

*21 To the one who is victorious, I will give the right*
*to sit with me on my throne, just as I was victorious and sat*
*down with my Father on his throne. 22 Whoever has ears,*
*let them hear what the Spirit says to the churches."*

The word Laodicea means "judgment of the people."
Metaphysically, it stands for human judgment. Judgment is our
faculty of discerning, evaluating, and making decisions. It is not
surprising that the Christ Mind has very little praise to give this
church in its present state. All that is said to it is, "'I know your
works...'" Even though this is but scant praise, at least it is
something. It indicates that at least we are "working" to develop
better judgment. There is obviously much that is still wrong in our
human judgments, but at least the Christ Mind is aware that we
are working to improve it.[87]

*You are neither cold nor hot. Would that you were cold or*
*hot! So, because you are lukewarm, and neither cold nor*
*hot, I will spew you out of my mouth.*

---

[87] 3:15,16

The lukewarm state so criticized by the Christ Mind symbolizes human reluctance to make decisions of either yea, yea, or nay, nay. It pertains to the fear many persons have to avail themselves of opportunities for choice and freedom of choice. It also includes the strange sort of reluctance some people have toward the fact that they are free to decide where to connect their sense of I AM. Too often we wait until someone or something outside ourselves tells us how to discern, what evaluation to make, and what decision we should make. This keeps our judgment faculty (church of Laodicea) in a non-creative (lukewarm) state. The Christ Mind indicates that for purposes of further spiritual unfoldment, this is unsatisfactory.[88]

> *For you say, I am rich, I have prospered, and I need nothing; not knowing you are that wretched, pitiable, poor', blind, and naked.*

This criticism of the Christ Mind toward human judgment refers to the fallacy of believing that our human judgment does not need further improvement ("'I am rich... I need nothing'") or that it is in any way fallible. No matter how good our judgment may seem to be, human judgment is always in need of improvement. In our human judgments, we need constant light from higher levels of being. That higher level is the Christ Mind, which needs to enter into our human judgment. The Christ Mind is always willing to do this. It is symbolized in these words:[89]

> *Behold, I stand at the door and knock; if any one hears my voice and opens the door, I will come in to him and eat with him, and he with me.*

---

[88] 3:17
[89] 3:20

If we want the illumination of divine guidance in our decision making, we need but acknowledge our willingness and ask for that guidance. If we open our minds and hearts to it, it will enter.[90]

> He who conquers, I will grant him to sit with me on my throne, as I myself conquered and sat down with my Father on his throne.

In Bible symbolism, a throne stands for a state of using good judgment. We are told here by the Christ Mind that if we want to sit on the throne (attain a high state of good judgment) we should remember that at any time we are discerning, evaluating, or making decisions, we should first take time to ask for the light of Christ to enter our judgment faculty (church of Laodicea) and work through us to illumine and guide us. If we do so, the Christ Mind will not fail us.

The church of Laodicea pertains to the seventh or crown chakra. It is traditionally associated with the pineal gland. Jesus gives an interesting description about this church. He states:[91]

> And unto the angel of the church of the Laodiceans write; These things say the Amen, the faithful and the true witness, the beginning of the creation of God; I know thy works, that thou are neither cold nor hot: I would that thou were cold or hot. So then because thou art lukewarm, I will spew thee out of my mouth.

It is said that when one opens the crown chakra you enter into enlightenment or cosmic consciousness and true union with

---

[90] 3:21
[91] 3:14-16

God. Before the opening of this chakra, it is neither hot nor cold. In other words, since this is the highest spiritual center of the body, when it is closed it is essentially inactive or dead. Therefore Jesus describes it as lukewarm, which is a temperature that really isn't desirable or useful for anything—it's potential is in danger of being completely discarded if it is not awakened. It is also interesting to note that Jesus doesn't admonish this church to further develop or purify any special qualities. That's because this spiritual center is either active or it isn't. Either you're in communion with God or you're not. Consider Jesus' next statement about the church of Laodicea:[92]

> *"Because thou sayest, I am rich, and increased with goods, and have need of nothing; and knowest not that thou art wretched, and miserable, and poor, and blind, and naked...*

Jesus is basically comparing this church to the same state of being that Adam and Eve were in as they were expelled from the Garden of Eden. They were naked, miserable, seemingly wretched, and had died spiritually. This makes complete sense; the death that God promised would come to man through the eating of the tree of knowledge was a spiritual death where spiritual wholeness was compromised for the sake of experience. Until this chakra is opened we cannot see this. We are essentially blind to spiritual wholeness and union with God until enlightenment is directly experienced. This explains a very misunderstood scripture:[93]

> "I have said ye are Gods; and all of ye children of the most High. But ye shall die like men, and fall like one of the princes".

---

[92] 3:17
[93] Psalm 82:6-7

How can one essentially be a God but still die like a man? The answer is simple: although we are all essentially a God since we come from spiritual wholeness, we shall still die like men unless this spiritual center is awakened by His Holy Spirit (kundalini). And we fall like princes because even though the prince has a right to inherit his father the king's throne, an early death may take that opportunity away. Similarly we all have the right to experience wholeness and communion with God, but when we fail to raise kundalini, we will simply reincarnate after physical death. This is like the falling of a prince who had the opportunity to inherit it all, but it never came to fruition.

A few verses later Jesus states to the Laodiceans:[94]

> "I counsel thee to buy of me gold tried in the fire (kundalini or Holy Spirit), that thou mayest be rich; and white raiment, that thou mayest be clothed, and that the shame of thy nakedness does not appear...

Adam and Eve did not feel shame in their nakedness when they walked in spiritual wholeness with God. They only became ashamed (had knowledge of their separation from God) once they had partaken of knowledge gained through experience. Remember, this is referring to a spiritual state, not a literal naked body. When energy rises up the spine and into the brain, there will be no more spiritual blindness to our true nature. We will be spiritually naked again without shame, because the nakedness of Adam and Eve before the fall represented purity and freedom from the lower nature of the mind. You will also be rich, not with material goods, but with true spiritual awareness.

---

[94] 3:18

# Chapter 13 –A Scene in Heaven

I.     Major Points
   - a. Metaphysical significance of God designated as "one".
   - b. Metaphysical meaning of the twenty-four elders.
   - c. Metaphysical meaning of the four beasts around the throne.
   - d. Metaphysical meaning of the four horsemen.

II.     Readings
   - a. From your own metaphysical understanding, explain the statement, "ONE seated on the throne."
   - b. List the four beasts and tell what each stands for in human nature,
   - c. What does the book with the seven seals stand for?
   - d. Why is only the Lamb worthy to open the seven seals of the book?
   - e. List the four horsemen and tell what each stands for.

III.     Questions
   - a. Revelation 4:1-6:8
   - b. Be Ye Transformed 219-226

*At once I was in the spirit, and lo, a throne stood in heaven, with one seated on the throne!"*[95]

Here is the great symbol which describes the sense of the presence of God. It is one. Just one. Not one this, or one that, but one itself! This requires metaphysical thinking for comprehension.

---

[95] 4:2

God is one but not in the sense of one object, one person, or one being. God is one in the true meaning of oneness itself (some persons refer to this as "Allness," but that is not quite the same thing; almost, but not quite.) God is not like the numerical digit 1, because in arithmetic the digit 1 can be followed by 2, 3, etc. This is not so of God. God is one without anything coming before or after.

> And he who sat there appeared like jasper and carnelian, and round the throne was a rainbow that looked like an emerald.[96]

The author equates the God presence with precious jewels and a rainbow. What distinguishes precious jewels and rainbows is their relationship to light. Precious jewels and rainbows have the appearances they have because of the effects of light. Without the radiance of light, we could not perceive the preciousness of jewels nor the beauty of a rainbow. Equating this idea with the description of the God presence, we are able to perceive God's presence only as there is light in our consciousness. Light is the biblical symbol of living intelligence and spiritual awareness.

> Round the throne were twenty-four thrones, and seated on the thrones were twenty-four elders, clad in white garments, with golden crowns upon their heads.[97]

Metaphysically the twenty-four elders symbolize the twelve powers functioning in a manner which seems to double their effectiveness. When we are in a strong sense of awareness of God's presence, our twelve powers have a powerful beneficial action on our own inner nature, and outwardly into our life

---

[96] 4:3
[97] 4:4

conditions and affairs. This two-fold direction of their benefits is symbolized in the number twenty-four.

Also, when our twelve powers are being utilized in worshipping God, they become imbued with pure power ("clad in white garments"), and they increase greatly in value to our spiritual unfoldment (wore crowns of gold). Also, they find expression through us in a very stable and mature manner (elders).

> ... and before the throne there is as it were a sea of glass, like crystal. And round the throne on each side of the throne, are four living creatures, full of eyes in front and behind..."[98]

To be "before the throne" means to be in a high state of good judgment. When we are using good judgment, there extends into our future an unlimited area of pure potentialities of good. This is the symbolism of the sea of glass and crystal. The sea stands for unlimited possibilities. Glass and crystal stand for purity.

"Eyes in front and behind" refers to the powers of foresight and hindsight. These are possessed by the four beasts mentioned. The four beasts represent the four main aspects of human nature.[99] They are:

- "like a lion"--physicality, the physical aspect of man, the physical body.
- "like an ox"--subjective and emotional nature of man, the emotional or astral body.
- "With the face of a man"--mental or intellectual nature of man, mental body.
- "like a flying eagle"--inspirational and intuitive nature of man, etheric body.

---

[98] 4:6
[99] 4:7

# Chapter 14 – The Book with Seven Seals

This chapter introduces us to the book sealed with seven seals. There is consternation in heaven because no man was yet able to lift the seals and open the book to read it. We are told that only the Lamb is found worthy to take the book and open the seals.

The book symbolizes full self-understanding and self-mastery. The seals on the book represent barriers to the process of self-understanding. Most people are not yet capable of gaining full insight into themselves because of the presence of certain mental and emotional "blocks" (seals).

The Lamb represents the gentle, kind, and forgiving nature of our Christ Self. Christ is totally harmless; all powerful, but harmless. Only through this attitude, symbolized as the Lamb, can any person gain the insights necessary to full self-understanding (open the seals).

## Opening the Seven Seals – Revelation 6

The opening of the seven seals by the Lamb symbolizes the gaining of insights leading to full self-understanding and self-discipline. Each seal that is opened represents the gaining of another step of insight into the inner workings of our own human nature.

> And I saw, and behold, a white horse, and its rider had a bow; and a crown was given to him, and he went out conquering and to conquer.[100]

The white horse and rider stand for our spiritual aspirations, based upon our understanding of Truth, motivated by

---

[100] 6:2

our commitment to Spirit. This comes first, and it overcomes all obstacles (went out to conquer).

> And out came another horse, bright red; its rider was permitted to take peace from the earth, so that man should slay one another; and he was given a great sword."[101]

The red horse and rider stand for our human tendency toward violence. Red is the color that symbolizes passion, and violence is one of the most common expressions of passion. This is still a quite active tendency in human nature. All wars among nations are a collective manifestation of this individual trait.

> ... and I saw, and behold, a black horse, and its rider had a balance in his hand; and I heard what seemed to be a voice . saying 'A quart of wheat for a denarius, and three quarts of barley for a denarius; but do not harm oil and wine![102]

The black horse and rider stand for the human tendency toward materialist greed and anxiety. When we read the words which the voice speaks in regard to this black horse and rider, we have a perfect illustration of this tendency. Materialistic greed and anxiety always make a fuss about possessions and profits. It is significant that black is the most opaque of colors, and materialistic anxiety is the most opaque of emotions in human nature.

> And I saw, and behold, a pale horse, and its rider's name was Death, and Hades followed him; and they were given power over a fourth of the earth, to kill with sword and

---

[101] 6:4
[102] 6:5-6

*with famine and with pestilence and by wild beasts of the earth."[103]*

The pale horse and rider stand for the habit of fear in general (pale), and also the belief in the inevitability of death (pale). Fear and belief in death are causing a drain of substance and vitality from our natures (pale). Death is the most misunderstood phenomenon in human experience. Until the Truth concerning it is perceived, mankind will continue to fear it. What we fear, we believe in. What we believe in, we hold in mind. What we hold in mind manifests after its kind.

*When he opened the fifth seal, I saw under the altar the souls of those who had been slain for the word of God and for the witness they had borne; they cried out with a loud voice, 'O Sovereign Lord, holy and true, how long before thou wilt judge and avenge our blood on those who dwell upon the earth?[104]*

The vision under the fifth seal symbolizes something which occupies a large part in the sub-consciousness of most persons: old disappointments and unhappy memories of being mistreated. These memories in us want to be assured that God's law of divine justice works. They want to be released from our subconscious (under the altar).

*Then they were each given a white robe and told to rest a little longer, until the number of their fellow servants and their brethren should be complete, who were to be killed as they themselves had been."[105]*

---

[103] 6:8
[104] 6:9-10
[105] 6:11

These words spoken to those under the altar constitute the assurance from the Christ Mind that God's law of divine compensation (justice) is always working, no matter how things may outwardly seem. All shall receive justice and right compensation under divine law. No good effort remains unrewarded. No unjust treatment remains uncompensated for. Even unhappy memories can be transformed into useful experience.

> When he opened the sixth seal, I looked, and behold, there was a great earthquake. ...[106]

The imagery of this sixth vision is so complex that it seems to defy point-by-point analysis. But, in general, it symbolically describes the continuation of the process of God's law of divine justice and compensation being fulfilled.

Many of our greatest rewards and compensations start out as seeming chaos and confusion (earthquake). But often, in reality, things are not shaking apart and getting worse, but they are shaking into new relationships in order to get better. Many of the "earthquakes" in our lives are really preludes for blessings, preludes to success.

> Then I saw another angel ascend from the rising of the sun, with the seal of the living God ... saying, 'Do not harm the earth or the sea or the trees, till we have sealed the servants of our God upon their foreheads.' And I heard the number of the sealed, a hundred and forty-four thousand sealed, out of every tribe of the sons of Israel."[107]

---

[106] 6:12
[107] 7:2-4

The twelve tribes of Israel symbolize the twelve spiritual faculties of man. The "seal of God" symbolizes the identity of a divine idea. The twelve faculties originate as divine ideas--144,000 is twelve times twelve, followed by three zeros. Zeros always symbolize "unlimited or unspecified." Here we have reference to the perfected human consciousness, which would be the twelve faculties combined and blended and integrated so that they, in a sense, "multiply one another to an unlimited degree (144,000)."

> Then one of the elders addressed me, saying, 'Who are these, clothed in white robes, and whence have they come?' I said to him, 'Sir, you know. ' And he said to me, 'These are they who have come out of the great tribulation; they have washed their robes and made them white in the blood of the Lamb. Therefore are they before the throne of God, and serve him day and night within his temple; and he who sits upon the throne will shelter them with his presence. They shall hunger no more, neither thirst any more... For the Lamb in the mi'dst of the throne will be their shepherd, and he will guide them to springs of living waters; and God will wipe away every tear from their eyes.[108]

The great majority of human tears are shed over regrets, guilts, and hurt feelings. Countless tears have been, and are still being shed for these causes. As a person grows in spiritual understanding, he begins to realize more and more that such tears are not as necessary as he once thought they were. He finds fewer occasions for tears. And when he comes into the fullness of understanding of the meaning of Christ within, he ceases further tears. In this manner it can be said that "God will wipe away every tear."

---

[108] 7:13-17

*When the Lamb opened the seventh seal, there was silence in heaven for about half an hour.*[109]

This is the culmination of the opening of the seven seals. This final step in the process of self-discovery is the realization of the meaning of becoming inwardly still and silent.

Knowing how to enter the true silence is usually one of the final things a person learns to do in his efforts to attain self-understanding and self-mastery. The ability to become inwardly still and silent is a mark of real attainment in development of spiritual consciousness. Silence begins with the quieting of all inner mechanical talking. It is a conscious, willing merging of self with the great silent principle of Being.

All ideas and principles are, "in the beginning," silence or light. But in order to be brought into expression and become manifest, they are brought into the realm of vibration, which is the realm formed by the power of the Word. The power of the Word produces expressions and manifestations of silent ideas and principles. But all ideas and principles originate and reside in the silence.

**Afflictions on the Earth**

| | |
|---|---|
| Revelation 8:7 Hail and fire, mixed with blood, fall upon earth and burn much of its vegetation. | Revelation 8:8 A third of the seas turn into blood. |
| Revelation 8:10-11 A star called Wormwood falls into the waters of the earth and turns the waters bitter. | Revelation 8:12 Much of the earth is enveloped in total darkness. |

---

[109] 8:1

| Revelation 9:3-6 A plague of stinging locusts torments mankind for five months. | Revelation 9:17 An army of monstrous creatures riding fire-breathing horses ride over the earth, killing a third of its inhabitants. |
| --- | --- |

These strange and disturbing visions symbolize the various aspects of what we view as earthly suffering in general. No explanation is given as to why these afflictions occur. No justification is offered. It is a mystery. It just seems to happen.

The same appears to be the case concerning earthly suffering in general. For most persons, there is not a satisfactory explanation as to why we suffer. There are explanations as to what causes suffering, and what kind of suffering is endured, but no real answer as to WHY. There seems no real justification for much of it. To most people, earthly suffering, on the whole, is a big mystery with no logical explanation. Like the afflictions in chapters eight and nine of Revelation, it just seems to happen.

It is important to realize that when the word "WHY?" is used in connection with questioning earthly suffering, it does not mean the same as, "How did it happen?" or "What caused it?" The word WHY is asking for a "good reason" or a "useful justification."

There are some further details concerning these visions of earthly suffering which are interesting to note:

(1) They are all temporary disasters. None affect the earth permanently. This is true of all general suffering. It is always temporary. Suffering may be a part of a cycle within a person's life, but it does not become all of a person's life. A person's life is eternal, but nothing that occurs as a part of a person's life is eternal. Events and conditions are always temporary, including all forms of suffering.

(2) These visions describe only part of the Earth and its inhabitants to be afflicted at any given time. This fact symbolizes an important metaphysical point. Only a certain part of a person's

being can suffer; not one's entire being. And only a portion of one's existence can be afflicted at any given time; not one's whole life. This may seem scant comfort, but at least it offers some comfort. Forms of earthly suffering, such as pain, disappointment, depression, anxiety, grief, lack, etc.; even though these hurt part of the man (a third of the earth), they do not and cannot harm the whole man. The Real Self of a person is always higher and greater than any part of himself that is suffering. And, eventually, new good can be brought forth even from suffering.

# Chapter 15 – The Angel and the Little Book

I.     Major Points
    a.  Metaphysical meaning of the souls under the altar.
    b.  Metaphysical significance of the earthquake under the 6th seal.
    c.  Metaphysical significance of "God will wipe away every tear."
    d.  Metaphysical significance of silence under the 7th seal.
    e.  Implications of afflictions and earthly suffering in general.

II.    Readings
    a.  Revelation 6:9-9:21
    b.  Be Ye Transformed 226-236

III.    Questions
    a.  Metaphysically, what do the souls under the altar stand for in human nature?
    b.  What does the earthquake under the 6th seal symbolize?
    c.  What is the metaphysical symbolism of the number 144,000?
    d.  From your own metaphysical understanding, comment upon the fact that SILENCE is under the 7th seal.
    e.  Should we try to justify and explain earthly suffering? If not, what should we attempt to do about it?

*Then the voice which I had heard from heaven spoke to me again, saying, 'Go, take the scroll which is open in the hand of the angel who is standing on the sea and on the land.' So*

*I went to the angel and told him to give me the little scroll; and he said to me, 'Take it and eat; it will be bitter to your stomach, but sweet as honey in your mouth.' And I took the little scroll from the hand of the angel and ate it; it was sweet as honey in my mouth, but when I had eaten it my stomach was made bitter.*[110]

The little scroll stands for the letter and the theory of metaphysical Truth teachings. In the form of a body of knowledge which can be learned, it is symbolized as a scroll in an angel's hand, which can be "eaten." In this form (knowledge of letter of Truth) it makes a sweet impression on our minds.

But knowledge of Truth must become digested into consciousness (in the stomach) in order to be put to work in one's life. It is here that the bitterness can be felt. Just learning the knowledge about spiritual healing can be a "sweet" experience. Needing a healing is a bitter thing. And using Truth to attain healing can sometimes prove to be rather a bitter effort. The same is true concerning forgiveness, letting go, non-resistance, etc.

It comes as somewhat of a pleasant surprise to many Truth students to eventually learn that it is not good for life to be all sweet. As one advances in spiritual understanding, he realizes that "bitterness" is just as valid and useful a part of life experience as "sweetness" is.

**Additional Notes**

After dealing with the interpretation of Revelation up to this point, a student might understandably get a bit weary with so much reference to difficulties and suffering. At this point it might be well to remind ourselves that the book of Revelation is a symbolic book, highly symbolic. It deals with the continued growth and unfoldment of our souls after we have come into the

---

[110] 10:8-10

way of truth as revealed by Jesus.. What this strange book has to tell us is that there are certain things a person can learn, accept, and understand only after he or she has made a serious commitment to Spirit.

For a time, most souls go through cycles of existence in which the goal of all their efforts is simply to get what they think they want, and avoid as much trouble and pain as is humanly possible. This can be the goal of life for many persons. Some may spend whole lifetimes never growing beyond this goal.

But some persons grow beyond this point and begin to see that self-seeking and finding ease and pleasure are not the highest goals to seek in life. Many Truth students come to realize that spiritual understanding is the most worthwhile of all goals. Then the direction of that person's life begins to turn away from certain past preoccupations and grows into new realizations.

In studying metaphysical Bible interpretation, we are attempting to learn and understand Truth which will take us out of many of the old habits and limitations of mechanical existence. While we know that the nature of life, the essence of life, and the purpose of life are good, we also reconcile ourselves to the fact that there are many factors yet within life which we still react to as not good. And it is to help us receive more light on certain of these factors that our Bible, and especially the book of Revelation, so often deals with difficult or unpleasant subjects.

## The two Witnesses – Revelation 11:3-12

This section deals with the "two witnesses" who are killed by "the beast that ascends from the bottomless pit." They are dead for three and a half days, but come back to life and go "up to heaven in a cloud.".

The meaning of the two witnesses has to be something which illustrates of character of bearing witness, or giving testimony to something concerning the Christ within. Yet they also have to be something that can be temporarily killed or suppressed in us by uprisings of negativity (beast ascending from the bottomless pit). Yet they are things which always spring back to 'life again in us.

Two things about the human soul which seem to fit into this symbolism would certainly be:

Good intentions.

Compassionate attitudes.

These two factors in consciousness, when alive and working, bear witness for us and give testimony for us that we are serious in our commitment to Spirit, and to our faith in God. But when sudden uprisings of negativity (beast) come from that mysterious, unexplainable "somewhere" (bottomless pit), very often these two factors in us become its first victims. Our good intentions and our compassionate attitudes go "dead."

But they refuse to stay dead! "But after the three and a half days a breath of life from God entered them, and they stood up on their feet. ... Then they heard a loud voice from heaven saying to them, 'Come up hither!1 And in the sight of their foes they went up to heaven in a cloud.[111]

Good intentions that are based on knowledge of Truth never die. Also, compassionate attitudes that are based on knowledge of Truth never die. Negativity that seems to come from nowhere may seem to wipe them out for a while, but they always return to life. As they return to life in us, they always become stronger. And they also resume a larger and more important place in our lives.

---

[111] 11:11-12

# Chapter 16 – The Beast and the Bottomless Pit

I. Major Points
   a. Metaphysical meaning of the little scroll that tastes sweet but becomes "bitter in the stomach."
   b. The primary purpose for metaphysical Bible interpretation.
   c. Metaphysical meaning of the two witnesses.
   d. The metaphysical meaning of the refusal of the two witnesses to remain dead after they were killed.

II. Readings
   a. Revelation 10:1-11:19
   b. Be Ye Transformed 236-239

III. Questions
   a. Why is what the little scroll stands for "sweet as honey in the mouth" but "bitter in the stomach?"
   b. What should be our primary goal in our study of Truth, and especially in metaphysical Bible interpretation?
   c. What do the two witnesses stand for in human nature?
   d. How are the two witnesses sometimes killed? Why do they refuse to stay dead?

**The Beast and the Bottomless Pit – Revelation 11:7**

Who and what is this "beast that ascends from the bottomless pit?" What is it that temporarily kills our two witnesses and causes so much anguish and harm? The beast of Revelation is the metaphysical symbol of negativity and violence still in existence in human nature.

Where does this negativity come from? In Revelation, it is symbolized as a "bottomless pit."

There is no bottom to it, which means there is no basis of reality to it. It is an endless hole, which means there is no real substance to it. Figuratively speaking, it is "nothing" coming from "nowhere." Yet it does manifest; it has its terminus point at three dimensional existence on Earth. The paradox is that it has no starting point, but it has an ending point, which is the realm of outer appearance.

Perhaps a summing up could be: The bottomless pit symbolizes the enigma of unreality brought into an appearance of reality, of nothingness being cast into a mold of somethingness. It is an age-old mystery. And the mystery is not solved by simply saying, "It doesn't exist." The beast does exist, but not for much longer!

The beast in Revelation stands for generalized evil or error in human experience. It is the greatest mystery and most infuriating paradox in human thinking. No one has ever been able to explain it. Some have tried to "explain it away" by simply claiming that "there ain't no such thing." But intelligence knows better. It exists. Our greatest authority on things metaphysical and Spiritual is Jesus Christ. Jesus only goes so far as to say this about "the devil": "a liar and the father of lies." (John 8:44) Jesus does not say that it does not exist. He says that it exists as a lie which produces other lies.

Further on in Revelation, there are additional references to this paradox:

- Revelation 17:8 "The beast that you saw was, and is not, and is to ascend from the bottomless pit and go to perdition... it was and is not and is yet to come."
- Revelation 17:11 "As for the beast that was and is not, it is... and it goes to perdition."

All this strange, seeming double-talk is actually illustrating one of the most subtle and difficult ideas for human thinking to comprehend. Evil, error, sin, and negativity (beast) come out of unreality (bottomless pit) and eventually must go back into ineffectiveness (perdition). It is the energy generated by the mind of man which gives temporary form to evil for a time (beast that was), but this is not permanent (yet is not). Therefore, even when negativity is being formed into temporary existence, it is a part of the process what will take it back into the nothingness from whence it came.

It is very important to remember that all we are dealing with here take place in our consciousness.

> *And a great portent appeared in heaven, a woman clothed with the sun, with the moon under her feet, and on her head a crown of twelve stars; she was with child and she cried out in her pangs of birth ("travailing in birth" KJV), in anguish for delivery.[112]*

Here we are presented with the idea of "pangs of birth" or "travail," which refers to the experience of productive or useful suffering. The woman stands for our illumined feeling nature that is committed to things spiritual. The child she is to deliver refers to our bringing forth a higher, finer development of our own nature.. To successfully become a finer and better person often originates with a feeling of "travail" or useful suffering. This is never agonizing, nor is it ever unbearable. It is of short duration, and it resolves into the most rewarding of all human accomplishments, the new birth, or "becoming a better human being."

> *And the dragon stood before the woman who was about to bear a child, that he might devour her child when she brought it forth.[113]*

---

[112] 12:1-2
[113] 12:4

The habits of negativity and violence in human nature constantly appear as threats to our efforts at self-improvement and spiritual unfoldment. Each new birth shortens the days of the "ascendency of the beast," so it assumes the role of enemy toward our own self-improvement.

> ...she brought forth a male child, one who is to rule all the nations with a rod of iron, but her child was caught up to God and to his throne, and the woman fled into the wilderness, where she has a place prepared by God, in which to be nourished for one thousand two hundred and sixty days.[114]

Once our new birth process begins, it will continue. Error and negativity may try to interfere, but they cannot prevail. Divine law gives our feeling nature protection and strength to enable us to continue this great process of self-evolution into higher consciousness. The woman (our feeling nature) gives birth to the male child (improved self) and is under the laws of divine guidance and divine protection throughout and after the event.

> ... who is like the beast, and who can fight against it?"[115]

Error and negativity can assume a bewildering number and variety of shapes and forms in our human experience. We often tend to evaluate the seriousness of an error by the form it assumes. But this leads to many false conclusions. Error is simply error. Negativity is simply negativity. Regardless of the form it assumes, or the numbers involved in its appearances, it is always overcome by truth thinking. Error thinking believes in "safety in

---

[114] 12:5-6
[115] 13:4

numbers," but Truth thinking realizes that all safety and strength lie in one source of help, which is God.

The "beast worshippers" represent a strange tendency in human nature. Human thinking can become strongly impressed and influenced by the vast number of appearances of error and negativity in the world. So much so that, in a sense, a person may begin to "worship" it, for the reason that he may believe that it is dangerous not to. Large numbers in outer appearances have a widespread hypnotic effect on people.

> *This calls for wisdom: let him who has understanding reckon the number of this beast, for it is a human number, its number is six hundred and sixty-six.*[116]

Error is symbolized by the number 666. Six is twelve divided. Twelve is the number symbolizing wholeness and completeness in the true sense of the word. (As contrasted to the number seven, which symbolizes completeness only on the manifest plane.) Six--half of twelve. Six--half whole, not whole, un-whole, unholy.

All sin, error, evil, and negativity are the result of lack of true understanding, with or without the accompaniment of malice or violence. Sin and evil are words which refer to any human attempt to negate divine ideas. Six, repeated three times, could symbolize repeated attempts to negate the meaning of twelve, the number symbolizing spiritual wholeness or rightness,

> *Then I looked, and lo, on Mount Zion stood the Lamb, and with him a hundred and forty-four thousand who had his name and his Father's name written on their foreheads.*[117]

---

[116] 13:18
[117] 14:1

This sentence refers to the "redeemed" part of our human nature. The meaning of 144,000 is directly the REVERSE of 666.

12--The twelve divine ideas implanted in the soul of man.

The twelve spiritual faculties or powers.

The wholeness and perfection with man's soul.

Man's spiritual nature.

12 X 12--The twelve powers combined with one another to expand and (144) multiply the effectiveness of each in a perfect pattern of wholeness.[118]

The spiritual nature of man expressing fully through the soul

> And another angel, a third, followed them, saying with a loud voice, 'If any one worships the beast and its image, and receives a mark on his forehead or on his hand, he also shall drink the wine of God's wrath, poured unmixed into the cup of his anger, and he shall be tormented with fire and sulphur in the presence of the holy angels and in the presence of the Lamb. And the smoke of their torment goes up for ever and ever; and they have no rest, day or night, these worshipers of the beast and its image, and whoever receives the mark of its name.[119]

In these verses, we have a classic example of the violent imagery of much of Revelation. It is in regard to that in us which has "the mark of the beast." This refers to all tendencies in our human nature to cling to error, sin, violence, and negativity. These simply cannot be allowed to remain in us indefinitely. They will always be detected and eventually cleansed from us (shall have

---

[118] Zeros following a number (any number of zeros) always symbolize unlimited but unspecified expression. 144,000 stands for our twelve powers combined with and multiplied by one another, giving expression to our spiritual potential in an unspecified and unlimited number of ways.
[119] 14:9-11

no rest day or night). The detecting of error is called "tormenting," and its dissolving and elimination are called "burning." This great, beneficial purification process within us is described as going on "forever and ever." It is part of eternal law.[120]

.

*And they assembled them at the place which is called in the Hebrew Armageddon.*[121]

This is the only time the name Armageddon is mentioned in the Bible. It is not listed at all in the Metaphysical Bible Dictionary. Yet, for some reason, it has assumed a place of tremendous importance in certain religious groups in our world today.

Metaphysically, Armageddon appears to stand for that place in consciousness where there is a struggle between our negative impulses and our faithfulness to Truth thinking. There is nothing unusual about this struggle, but it does occur daily in most persons.

---

[120] It is in passages such as this that taking the Bible literally may cause a person's metaphysical understanding to go "haywire." If this passage were talking about actual human beings going through an almost indescribable torment, we have a barbaric return to the Old God of revenge and cruelty. Revelation is not about such a concept of God. It is a metaphysical-symbolic vision of the eventual neutralizing and eliminating of sin and error from human nature

[121] 16:16

# Chapter 17 – The Downfall of Babylon

I.      Major Points
    a.  Symbolism of the beast and the bottomless pit.
    b.  The contradictory nature of the beast.
    c.  The metaphysical idea of "pangs of birth" or "travail."
    d.  The metaphysical meaning of the birth of a new male child.
    e.  Symbolism of the number 666.
    f.  The self-destructive nature of error and evil.

II.     Readings
    a.  Revelation 11:1-16:21
    b.  Be Ye Transformed 240-253

III.    Questions
    a.  Metaphysically, what does the beast stand for?
    b.  Give a metaphysical commentary on a "bottomless pit."
    c.  How are the "pangs of birth" or "travail" different from ordinary suffering?
    d.  What is the metaphysical meaning of the birth of a new male child?
    e.  What is the significance of the number 666?
    f.  What is the one point all metaphysical schools of thought agree upon in regard to error and evil?

These chapters deal in very fanciful imagery with the "heyday" and downfall of Babylon. The metaphysical significance of this is hinted at in these words: "... and on her forehead was written a name of mystery: "Babylon the Great, Mother of Harlots and of Earth's Abomination.[122]

The city of Babylon has almost the same metaphysical meaning as the character Jezebel. Both represent negative emotions. The word Babylon means "confusion; chaos; vanity; nothingness." These definitions describe our negative emotions, just as the meaning of Jezebel did.

Chapter seventeen describes Babylon as seductive, dangerous, harmful , and abominable. The same might be said for negative emotions in general. The "fornications" committed with her by the "kings of the earth" refer to those times when, in our human thinking, we have placed our sense of I AM into our negative emotions (fornication).

The downfall of Babylon described in chapter eighteen symbolizes the Truth that our negative emotional states (Babylon) and the results of those states (her fruits) must eventually come to an end. The products of negative emotions (abomination) shall be reduced to nothingness (ashes). Just as the physical planet (Earth) in Revelation shall be cleansed of the abominable city of Babylon, so shall our metaphysical planet (soul) be cleansed of abominable negative emotions.

> And the kings of the earth, who have committed fornication and were wanton with her, will weep and wail over her when they see the smoke of her burning."[123]

What is the significance of the fact that the kings of the Earth and the merchants bewail and lament the destruction of Babylon? Their laments began after an angel announced, "... Fallen, fallen is Babylon the great ....!"[124] This means that all negative emotional states must fail to survive. They may have a

---

[122] 17:5
[123] 18:9
[124] 18:2

great "heyday" in us while they last, but they cannot last. Every negative emotion carries its own seed of destruction, which is working even when it seems to have power over a person.

But what about the wailing and weeping by the kings of the Earth and the merchants? The "kings of the earth" and "merchants" stand for those parts of our human nature which still hold to the belief that there are desirable and worthwhile things to hold on to in negative emotions. These parts of our minds still believe that there is a serious loss when a negative emotion is given up or taken away. There is still something in human nature which prizes negativity and is reluctant to abandon it.

At one time, on the evolutionary ladder, it is probable that what we now experience as negative emotions were primitive levels of certain survival instincts. As such, they had validity and usefulness. But with the continuing of the evolution of consciousness, they have long served their old purpose and are no longer needed. They have now fulfilled their old role and are redundant and dangerous. Their energies need to be converted into more positive and useful forms in keeping with current evolutionary demands. When this is done within a person, it is called "redemption."

Revelation 19 mentions the forthcoming marriage of the Lamb and his bride, which is fulfilled in the finale of Revelation.

*Then I saw heaven opened, and behold, a sat upon it is called Faithful and True ..."*[125]

This is the reappearance of the white horse and rider mentioned earlier in the book, but this time the rider is named specifically (in chapter six he was not named). He is given the name Faithful and True. When we remember that in chapter six, his meaning was given as our spiritual aspirations and our

---

[125] 19:11

commitment to Spirit, this makes it quite appropriate that he be named Faithful and True. Faith and Truth in our consciousness are the origins of our spiritual aspirations and our willingness to commit our lives to things spiritual.

> And he seized the dragon, that ancient serpent, who is the new Devil and Satan, and bound him for a thousand years, and threw him into the pit, and shut it and sealed it over him, that he should deceive the nations no more, till the thousand years were ended. After that he must be loosed for a little while."[126]

> And when the thousand years are ended, Satan will be loosed from his prison."[127]

"Thousand," or any number of zeros following a number, is always the biblical numerical symbol designating unlimited or unspecified. This is a constant. In these statements, the author is referring through the symbolism to the fact that in our human existences, we seem always to have alternating and contrasting cycles and phases of events and experiences. The actual length of time of any cycle is unspecified (000) and may vary quite widely. But a cycle of activity of any sort is referred to as lasting a "thousand years," which does not mean 1,000 years of literal time, but simply as an unspecified period of time.

Satan bound a thousand years is symbolic of periods in our lives when negativity is not dominating our mental and emotional states. We enjoy a blessed sense of freedom, and we learn and grow quite rapidly during these periods.

But it seems that after each of these good cycles, the "ancient serpent" of negative impulse is let out again "for a little

---

[126] 20:2-3
[127] 20:7

while." This is merely a description of the type of fluctuation between positive and negative energy expressions, quite typical of all human nature and its pattern of evolution. There is nothing alarming or abnormal about this experience or fluctuating between positive and negative.

> ... and the devil who had deceived them was thrown into the lake of fire and sulphur where the beast and the false prophet were, and they will be tormented day and night for ever and ever."[128]

> Then death and hades were thrown into the lake of fire. This is the second death. ...[129]

> ... and if any one's name was not found written in the book of life, he was thrown into the lake of fire.[130]

These statements symbolize the processes within the soul of a person who has learned to control the lower, negative, Satanic factors in consciousness. Such a person gives top priority to expressions of his higher, Christ-like levels of consciousness. Such a soul is designated by the author as "he who shares in the first resurrection."[131]

In this soul, the drastic fluctuations between positive and negative subside. In this soul, there is more of the expressing of the twelve faculties in harmonious integration (the WHOLE consciousness). There is also a definite and permanent ability to distinguish between Truth and error. All error will be rejected and let go, consigned to a dissolving and purifying process carried out by spiritual judgment and spiritual elimination (lake of fire).

---

[128] 20:10
[129] 20:14
[130] 20:15
[131] 20:6

It is significant that the first two items to go into this final dissolving and purifying process are: "DEATH and HELL were thrown into the lake of fire." Death first; then Hell. Hell or Hades stands for useless, unnecessary suffering. And the concept of death now held in the minds of the majority of mankind is completely erroneous. It shall be done away with, along with hell. The lake of fire is not a symbol of punishment but of cleansing and elimination. Its fires are the reducing of negative forms of mental and emotional energy into the basic purity and harmless substance (ashes).

Then comes the next blessing. "... and if any one's name was not found written in the book of life, he was thrown into the lake of fire." This means doing away with anything that is not a real, legitimate, or useful part of life (not found written in the book of life). This means anything that is harmful, erroneous, useless for further progress, such as sickness, unhappiness, anxiety, fear, loneliness, boredom, hopelessness, hatred, hurt feelings, etc. These are not things "written into our book of life by the Christ Mind," so they shall be dissolved into elemental substance by the purifying processes of Spirit (lake of fire; fire of God).

**A New Heaven and a New Earth – Revelation 21-22**

Since these chapters conclude the book of Revelation, they constitute the climax of the Bible narrative as a whole. These chapters present a very special challenge to both serious students and casual readers, because they symbolically describe something which probably few persons, if any, have as yet experienced; a state of inner and outer well-being based upon a totally integrated consciousness of Truth.

Outwardly and literally these chapters consist of details about the new city of Jerusalem which comes down from heaven. Everything about the city is connected with the number twelve. The word Jerusalem means "habitation of peace." Metaphysically, it stands for an illumined spiritual consciousness. Such a consciousness produces total well-being, inwardly and outwardly, for the one who has attained it.

The number twelve is used lavishly in both chapters. In every descriptive detail concerning the new city we find the number twelve, the numerical symbol of wholeness and perfection:

- 12 gates.
- 12 angels at the gates.
- 12 foundations for the walls.
- 12 names of apostles written in the foundations.
- 12,000 stadia (furlongs, KJV) the measurement of the city.
- 144 (12 X 12) cubits as the measurement of the wall.
- 12 precious jewels on the foundations of the walls.
- 12 pearls as gates.
- 12 kinds of fruit on the tree of life.

The number twelve, as used in these final pages of Revelation, stands for inner and outer wholeness and perfection — perfect in expression as well as in being. Until in the final chapters, the number twelve has been used in the Bible in connection with potential perfection, possibility of perfection. Here it is being used as perfection in actualization and expression. This is something that is probably beyond the comprehension of human thinking as it exists today. We can probably only grasp it intuitively.

The climactic use of the symbolism of twelve is found in the twelve kinds of fruit on the tree of life.[132] The tree of life in Revelation is in contrast to the tree of life in Genesis. The Genesis tree of life is guarded by a cherubim with a flaming sword. This is to keep imperfect human nature (Adam after the "fall") from

---

[132] 22:2

gaining immortal life while in that imperfect state of consciousness. Such an eternal existence would be terrible for the one experiencing it.

The tree of life in Revelation is freely offered to all who are eligible to approach it. These are persons who have earned the New Jerusalem consciousness (full spiritual illumination). While the tree of life in Genesis provides eternal existence in limited material consciousness, the tree of life in Revelation provides unlimited eternal life in spiritual consciousness.

The twelve kinds of fruit on the tree symbolize the true inner realization of the nature and character of our twelve spiritual faculties. True eternal life is the harmonized and integrated awareness of and expression of the twelve powers of humankind as revealed by Jesus Christ:

- Faith
- Love
- Judgment
- Order
- Strength
- Power
- Imagination
- Understanding
- Zeal
- Will
- Elimination
- Life

Before Revelation ends, there are two very curious verses which might be taken in a number of ways. We shall not attempt to interpret them in this course, since it is not clear as to why they appear.

*I warn everyone who hears the words of the prophecy of this book: if any one adds to them, God will add to him the plagues described in this book, and if any one takes away from the words of the book of this prophecy, God will take away his share in the tree of life and in the holy city, which are described in this book.*[133]

Although we promised not to attempt to interpret these statements, one cannot help but speculate as to whether or not the writer might have been expressing some personal consternation over the fact that at the time of his writing there were no copyright laws!

But now, the very beautiful and appropriate ending of the book of Revelation and, therefore, the closing blessing from the Bible: "The grace of the Lord Jesus Christ be with all the saints. Amen.[134]

---

[133] 22:18-19
[134] 22:21

# Appendix I – Symbolism

## Churches and Chakras

| Church | Chakra - Gland | Seal |
|---|---|---|
| Ephesus | Base or Root - Gonads | 1 |
| Smyrna | Sacral - Ayden | 2 |
| Pergamos | Solar Plexus - Adrenals | 3 |
| Thyatira | Heart - Thymus | 4 |
| Sardis | Throat - Thyroid | 5 |
| Philadelphia | Third Eye - Pineal | 6 |
| Laodicea | Crown - Pituitary | 7 |

## Chapters 4-11 The Seals

| Symbol | Meaning |
|---|---|
| Paradise of God | The original consciousness of humanity before its incarnation |
| Tree of Life | The spiritual centers of the body or chakras, such as the heart and the pituitary, that becomes perfectly synchronized |
| Angel of the Church | The intelligent force governing a spiritual center within the body |
| Satan | The force of self-centeredness, self-gratification, self-indulgence, self-importance, self-righteousness, self-consciousness, self-glorification, self-delusion, self-condemnation, self, ego, the "false god," the "beast" Also known as the accuser. |
| Book of Life | The collective unconscious record (memory) of all souls |
| Earth | The physical body |
| Mountain of fire striking the Earth | The forces within the physical body which are constantly warring within |
| New Jerusalem | The superconscious mind awakened |
| Nakedness | The exposure of faults |
| Seven lamps | The wisdom of the seven spiritual centers within the body |

## Chapters 12-14 A Woman, a Dragon, Two Beasts and a Lamb

| Symbol | Meaning |
|---|---|
| Seven candlesticks, seven spirits | Perfection, the divine number |
| Six | Imperfection, the number for humanity |
| Mark of the beast | The unevolved animalistic force within humans |
| Mark of the lamb | The evolved divine force within humans |
| 666 | The unevolved animalistic force affecting the nature of humans - (body, soul, spirit) |

## Chapters 15-18 Seven Angels, Seven Vials and a Prostitute

| Symbol | Meaning |
|---|---|
| Seven plagues | The purification and tribulation experienced by souls in order to overcome negative karma |
| Vials of God's wrath | Karma, eye for an eye, sowing and reaping, the consequences of our negative acts |
| Armageddon | The spiritual conflict within humans |
| False prophet | Self-delusion |

## Chapters 19-22 Rejoicing, Bottomless Pits, a New Heven and a New Earth

| Symbol | Meaning |
|---|---|
| Marriage of the Lamb | The union of the body and soul with the Christ consciousness |
| Word of God | The Gnostic "logos," the Christ consciousness, the fully evolved pattern for humanity |
| Lake of Fire | The subconscious mind's area of repression, the "id"[135] |
| The first resurrection | The reincarnation of advanced souls to Earth |
| Gog and Magog | Worldly influences |
| The dead in judgment | Reincarnating souls |
| Hell | Remorse, self-condemnation, guilt and frustration |
| The second death | The destruction of all man-made unevolved conditions |

---

[135] Id, ego, and super-ego are the three parts of the psychic apparatus defined in Sigmund Freud's structural model of the psyche; they are the three theoretical constructs in terms of whose activity and interaction our mental life is described. According to this model of the psyche, the id is the set of uncoordinated instinctual trends; the super-ego plays the critical and moralizing role; and the ego is the organized, realistic part that mediates between the desires of the id and the super-ego.[1] The super-ego can stop one from doing certain things that one's id may want to do.

| 12 tribes of Israel, 12 gates, 12 angels, 12 foundations, 12 disciples | The 12 basic patterns of the human personality as revealed in the Zodiac |
| --- | --- |
| Temple of God | The superconscious mind, the Christ consciousness |
| New Jerusalem | The evolved soul in one-ness with divinity |

# Index

144,000, 95, 99, 108
666, 8, 107, 108, 111, 123
Adam and Eve, 85, 86
Afflictions, 97, 99
Amillennialism, 10, 11
Angel, 99, 122
Angels, 40
Antichrist, 9, 12
Apocalypse, 1, 2, 4, 8, 12, 13, 14, 15, 17, 18, 21
Armageddon, 2, 7, 109, 123
Aura, 30
Babylon, iii, 7, 9, 21, 111, 112
Base or Root Chakra, 31
Beast, iii, 7, 101, 102, 103, 104, 105, 106, 107, 108, 111, 115, 122, 123
Book of Life, 122
Candlesticks (7), 123
Cayce, Edgar, 21
Chakras, 18, 29, 30, 31, 32, 33, 34, 35, 36, 45, 121
Churches, Seven, 40
Consciousness, 17, 24, 33, 40, 44, 46, 49, 50, 51, 53, 59, 62, 65, 71, 76, 79, 84, 88, 95, 96, 100, 102, 105, 106, 109, 113, 114, 115, 116, 117, 118, 122, 124, 125

Crown Chakra, 36
Darby, John Nelson, 9
Eastern Orthodoxy, 12
Elders (24), 37, 87, 88, 89, 95
Energy Centers, 43
Ephesus, 3, 15, 38, 41, 42, 43, 44, 45, 121
Esoterist Views, 20
Fillmore, Charles, 24, 25, 49, 58
Futurist, 7, 8, 9
Gnostic, 20, 124
Haye, Tim, 9, 10
Heart Chakra, 33
Horse, Black, 92
Horse, Pale, 92, 93
Horse, Red, 92
James, i
Jerusalem, 7, 10, 11, 13, 74, 77, 78, 116, 118, 122, 125
Jews, 7, 13, 25, 48, 50, 51, 74, 76
Jezebel, 61, 63, 64, 65, 112
Lamps (7), 122
Laodicea, 3, 38, 81, 82, 83, 84, 85, 121
Lindsay, Hal, 9, 10
Marriage of the Lamb, 124
Messianic Prophecy, 12

Metaphysical Interpretation, 23

Metaphysical Views, 21

Midtribulationist, 8

Pergamon, 55

Pergamos, 59, 121

Philadelphia, 3, 38, 73, 74, 75, 76, 78, 121

Plagues (7), 123

Postmillennialism, 10, 12

Post-tribulationist, 9

Powers, Twelve, 88, 89, 108, 118

Premillennialism, 10

Preterism, 7

Pretribulationists, 8

Rapture, 12

Sacral Chakra, 32

Sardis, 3, 38, 67, 68, 71, 121

Satan, 2, 7, 10, 48, 50, 51, 56, 57, 59, 60, 62, 74, 76, 114, 122

Scroll, Little, 100, 103

Seals (7), 37, 87, 91, 96

Smyrna, 3, 38, 47, 48, 49, 50, 52, 53, 76, 121

Solar Plexus Chakra, 33

Soul, 20, 21, 23, 24, 28, 29, 31, 34, 40, 44, 45, 52, 58, 69, 102, 108, 112, 115, 123, 124, 125

St. John Chrysostom, 2

Substance, 49, 50, 51, 52, 53, 58, 93, 104, 116

Third Eye Chakra, 35

Throat Chakra, 34

Thyateira, 61, 62

*Tree of Life*, 43, 45, 117, 118, 119

Tribes (12), 95

Tribulation, 8, 9

Twelve, 41, 88, 89, 95, 105, 107, 108, 115, 116, 117, 118

Witnesses (2), 20, 101, 103

Made in the USA
Monee, IL
26 January 2022

89914935R00075